Musing
Mediterranean

Musing Mediterranean

Fun, Family, and Faraway Places Transform an Anxious Traveler

Beth Daigle

E. L. Marker
Salt Lake City

published by E. L. Marker, an imprint of
WiDō Publishing
Salt Lake City, Utah
widopublishing.com

Cover artist: Ken Bonin
Cover colorist: Stephen Pennimpede
Cover design: Steven Novak
Book design: Marny K. Parkin
Author photo: Emily O'Brien Photography

ISBN 978-1-947966-07-9

Printed in the United States of America

Contents

Introduction

I CAN'T TELL YOU HOW MANY TIMES I WAS ASKED "How was your trip?" after I returned from a summer 2012 family trip to Greece, Italy, and Turkey. It's a kind and innocent enough question, but I couldn't possibly give an answer to do this particular trip justice. This trip, this journey, changed who I was and who I wanted to be.

Sure, I wanted to tell anyone willing to listen all about the fun, fabulous, and even frightful things we experienced. But I always hesitated, knowing there was just too much to cover in any reasonable amount of time. I worried that any poor soul nice enough to ask about my "big vacation" would deeply regret their curiosity. There's nothing worse than looking into someone's eyes and realizing that they've glazed over in a state of vacation minutiae overload.

Although I knew this Mediterranean adventure was truly something special, I never did get the chance to tell anyone the whole story. I'm talking about the story that went much deeper than the beautiful buildings, delicious food, and European shopping we experienced.

This journey was one of firsts. It was my first two-week vacation, my first big family trip, and my first visit to Greece, Italy, and Turkey. It wasn't just physical, traveling from place to place, it was emotional. It brought about many personal revelations, as well as a renewed appreciation for travel that had been lost for a long time. More than discovering the wonders of three beautiful countries, this trip was about stepping outside my comfort zone and rediscovering the worldly traveler within.

1. Conflicted

OUR "BIG TRIP" WAS ABOUT TWO MONTHS AWAY. IT was all I could think about, and not in a good way. At about ten p.m., although it felt much later, I plopped down on my comfy bed at home, feeling spent. Not from physical exertion, but mental exhaustion. I was so tired from worrying about this trip that I was annoying myself. The pent-up stress was draining my energy. My body felt heavy and my head even more so. I had attempted to calm my nerves with just a couple, okay, maybe three, glasses of pinot grigio. I just wanted to relax, and it was pinot, for heaven's sake, barely a step above water.

But my soothing strategy had an unfortunate effect. Before I could shut my eyes and drift off to sleep, I began crying. Sobbing, really, like an overtired toddler, curled up in bed with my head in my pillow.

Tony, my husband of fifteen years, heard me through our bathroom door and flew into our dark bedroom asking, "What's the matter? What's going on?"

I moaned and muttered something like, "I don't know, I'm just afraid to go on this trip. Why can't we stay home?"

"You were fine a minute ago. What happened between then and now?"

Nothing had happened. My mild hysteria had been there all along, eating away at me and wearing me down. But, as I often do with things that make me uneasy, I put on a fearless facade and tried to pretend it wasn't happening. I wanted nothing more than to convince everyone, mostly myself, that flying eight hours from Boston, Massachusetts, to Rome, Italy, would be fine. Eight hours . . . dear God!

I wasn't always afraid of flying, but after September 11, 2001, I developed a phobia that became progressively worse. I recall watching the horrific events unfold on television, while cradling my firstborn, Julia. She was six months old. I was devastated thinking this was the kind of world the beautiful baby in my arms would have to grow up in. I called Tony, who was at his office in Boston, and insisted that he come home right away. I was panicked that Boston might be next. I remember feeling physically stunned as I stood glued to the television, chills running up and down my body. I didn't realize then it was my long-term emotional state that would be most deeply impacted.

I didn't lose anyone close to me that day. I can't imagine what I'd be like now if I had. I'd never been a trusting person, and I became even less so. I looked at almost everyone with skepticism, and the mere thought of travel by plane left me pensive and panic stricken. It didn't matter if the flight was short or long, overseas or cross-country—I didn't want to get on a plane. To those who say we can't live in fear, I agree, and I didn't want to, but my mind doesn't work like that. I couldn't unsee or unknow the dangers and risks that had pierced my psyche.

When I felt my fear of flying to Europe mount, I should have done something about it. But somehow, I felt addressing the fear would give it more strength. Although flying to Rome would not be the first plane ride I'd taken since 9/11, it would be the longest.

Short trips to Florida and Atlanta had come up and, despite my anxiety, I went. For whatever reason, I didn't want anyone to know how bad my fear had become. I would always do my best to divert my focus from anything having to do with getting on the plane. I tried turning my attention to joyful things, all in a ruse aimed at ensuring I didn't miss out on seeing the world.

What I did miss out on, however, was any clear memory of the trips I'd taken before I was emotionally ready. On the trip to Atlanta for my cousin's wedding and the other to Florida to join friends on a cruise departing from Fort Lauderdale, I was so preoccupied with preventing a freak out that I ended up in a total fog. I have no detailed recollection, to this day, of either of those trips. And, no, I did not self-medicate. It was just my brain shutting down in the face of a fear I wasn't adequately equipped to handle.

It's a shame, really, because at one time in my life, travel was a welcome treat. To see the world was something I craved. I was in my twenties—young, carefree, and full of energy. My earliest travel desires were satisfied with warm weather vacations to the Caribbean, Bermuda, and Aruba; I felt exotic. Business trips took me across America, affording me the pleasure of seeing and appreciating my own country; I felt cultured. Eventually, I would cross the pond and visit London and Paris. I had romanticized these cities in my mind since I was a teenager, and neither failed to impress; I felt well-traveled.

My ongoing love affair with Europe began then. In both London and Paris, more than any other places, I wanted to be both British and Parisian. I poked my nose into hole-in-the-wall eateries and quaint boutiques; I walked or took public transportation instead of cabs and spoke the language or lingo as best I could. This type of non-touristy travel became so important to me that when Tony and I opted for a restful honeymoon cruise to the Caribbean, it seemed more like an entrapment than a relaxing escape.

We were so young and energetic back then, we couldn't relax. We didn't want to relax. We were anxious and excited to experience island life and foreign lands. Lazing aboard a cruise ship simply didn't satisfy us. Even the plethora of midnight buffets, theater productions, deck activities and poolside parties didn't dull our anticipation for what was to come. Our sights were always set on the destination.

Back then, travel was so much more than a scheduled vacation. It was necessary for my personal fulfillment. Like a hungry puppy pulling on your pant leg, it felt like the travel bug would forever tug at me if I didn't give it the attention it deserved.

Those days are gone. I'm not sad about it, necessarily. It's just the way it is. Even without my delayed-onset fear of flying, travel has been pushed aside, in great part, because life got in the way.

Now in my forties, I have a supportive, hardworking husband, two beautiful daughters, Julia and Ally, a part-time writing career, and a beautiful home in an active community. Together, these wonderful things are all-consuming.

In the years after 9/11, Tony must have flown out to meet up with friends or go on business trips a dozen times. I always stayed home with the girls. Eventually, he stopped asking me to join. He knew what the answer would be, and he knew I couldn't handle it. Occasionally, he'd ask, "Don't you want to get away with some friends or your sister?" I always answered truthfully, "Not really." I was almost embarrassed by my lack of desire. While I could blame most of my missed travel opportunities on my aerophobia, that excuse didn't hold up when we were traveling by car, train, or boat.

One summer when we were going back and forth to our summer home in New Hampshire, I realized that I'd begun to resist these weekend getaways, too. What the heck was wrong with me? After a little self-analysis, I determined that venturing away from home, as a whole, was off-putting to me. Suddenly, the depth of my travel anxiety came into focus. Flying aside, it was also the packing, preparation, and lack of routine that made me want to pull my hair out.

I took a hard look at myself in the mirror and saw a textbook homebody staring back at me. How did this happen?

Yes, I was content in my home, my town, and my quaint little suburban neighborhood, and that's a good thing. But not so much that I shouldn't want to get away for a while. The fact that I would get homesick, with a nagging feeling that life as usual was going on without me, after about three days was utterly ridiculous. Life as usual isn't even all that interesting.

I really had to get my act together if I had any hope of making the most of my Mediterranean expedition.

Luckily, I had a staunch support system to help keep my mildly agoraphobic tendencies at bay. Tony refused to enable my hermit-like habits and insisted that we expose our daughters to the wonderful world that surrounds them. Tony loves to travel and while I wanted to do less of it, he wanted to travel more.

"If we don't travel with the kids now while they're young, we'll lose the chance. I want to see the world with them," he said.

Julia was eleven years old and Ally was nine, but I knew Tony was right. Soon enough they'd be teenagers. Their lives would get busier, and they'd probably be much less interested in spending time with their parents.

My friends didn't understand me either.

"How are you not more excited about getting away?" my friend Jen said one night while tossing dice at our neighborhood bunco game. "I would jump at any chance to get away from the monotony of suburban life for a day, never mind fourteen."

Bunco, by the way, is a fun little dice game that is the perfect excuse for a bunch of women to get together and drink wine.

I issued my standard response with the hope the conversation would go no further.

"I'm just not a big traveler. You know me—I like being home."

Honestly, I should have wanted to run screaming from the streets of suburbia. It's not as if the endless carting kids around, the busybody gossip, and dreadful keeping up with the Joneses is at all enriching. Yet, I stayed put as much as possible right in the middle of it until someone, usually Tony, knocked some sense into me. I finally acquiesced to a fourteen-day vacation with my entire family—my mother and father (the Thomases), my sister, brother-in-law, niece and nephew (the Kittlers), Tony, Julia, Ally, and me (the Daigles).

I looked at this first-ever attempt at group family travel in two ways: the cluster of the ten of us, ranging in age from nine to seventy-five, would be just the distraction I needed to help me forget my travel woes. Or, my worries would be compounded by the chaos that would likely ensue when a group of this size, personality, and various ages tried to come to an agreement on just about anything.

Organizing this kind of crowd was ambitious, even for Tony, who is a quintessential planner. He had a lot of work ahead of him to fill up a fourteen-day agenda, and he approached it with the same fervor as a teenage girl let loose in the mall with her parents' credit card.

Every once in a while, Tony's excitement would rub off on me, and I'd feel a flutter of happy anticipation about finally seeing the Mediterranean. Greece and Italy, in particular, had been calling my name for as long as I could remember. If the chance to go to either place had happened prior to 9/11, I'd have booked the earliest flight I could find.

I'm half Greek and half Italian, and visiting my ancestral countries for the first time was a special opportunity. Experiencing them with my sister and parents was something I'd always wanted to do. I had to get over whatever was holding me back. Fortunately, a trip of this magnitude would take a while to schedule and coordinate. I told myself I'd have plenty of time to get used to the idea and work out my "issues."

2. It's a Process

PLANNING A FOURTEEN-DAY EUROPEAN VACATION
for ten people is no easy task. For that reason, I chose to have
no part of it.

Tony, on the other hand, revels in planning. His personality is an interesting mix of type A businessman and fun-loving, life of the party. Somehow, he's managed to balance his dorky accountant side with his big guy, jock-like social side.

When I say big, Tony is six feet, two inches tall with broad shoulders and an athletic frame. He doesn't quite fit the physical stereotype most people have of an accountant, but he is very good at what he does.

Organization and life planning are, in fact, two of his strong points. I often wonder if Tony feels misunderstood. Anyone who knows him likes him because he's kind and thoughtful. But as the owner and founding partner of his tax consulting and advisory firm, he is often seen as serious and driven. Very few see his sensitive side. Truthfully, I rarely see it, but it's there.

He lost both his parents at an early age—his father when he was five and his mother when he was eighteen. I never met them, but it's clear they were a tight family. His and his two older sisters' lives were altered dramatically, but he prefers not to talk about it.

At eighteen, Tony was still in college. Losing his mother could have broken him, but instead it fueled his desire to succeed. His friends rallied around him and, in a way, replaced the family he'd lost. They also brought out his fun side, which is how I got to know him when we first met in our early twenties. He's still very close with each of those friends today. They became the brothers to each other that, interestingly, none of them had.

Unlike Tony, my upbringing was normal. I would say I was an average kid. I got good grades, not great, and followed the expected path through high school, college, and on to work. I studied business in school and worked in marketing until I had children. I was never passionate about my career because, while I always wanted to succeed, I didn't have the gut instinct to get there. I lean more toward creative pursuits. I enjoy art, writing, gardening, and entertainment. I live more for the moment than the future. This is why Tony was the perfect person to plan the trip and leave me out of it.

The planning phase of our Mediterranean vacation, which was a ten-day cruise preceded by a few extra days in Rome, began one and a half years prior to our departure date.

It all began with a routine haircut for Tony. As he does every month or so, he stopped in to see his barber, Sam (actually Sandra, her initials are S.A.M.). She had been cutting his hair for eight years, and for that same amount of time, she'd been sharing with him stories about her worldly travels.

Sam is a cruising aficionado. On this day while she trimmed Tony's hair, she chatted about her most recent cruise to the Mediterranean. At the first snip of her scissors, Tony was tuned in to her travel tales as though he were listening to a breaking newsflash. I imagine Sam must have described her experience in the most tempting way because Tony could not wait to replicate her every move. Not only did he come home looking particularly tidy up top, but he was on a mission to lock down our own itinerary as soon as possible. I had never seen anyone so enthusiastic when returning home from errands and a haircut.

"Girls, we are going to the Mediterranean," Tony announced to Julia, Ally, and me as soon as he walked in the door.

"How did getting your hair cut turn into a trip to the Mediterranean?" I asked.

"Yes!" Ally cheered. "When are we going and where's the Mediterranean?"

"Okay, everyone slow down a second." I figured I'd better put a stop to this before my overzealous family bamboozled me into something I had no idea about.

I'm the queen of being guilted into doing stuff when I'm the only naysayer of the group.

"Listen, it's going to be great," Tony said. "We'll invite your parents and the Kittlers, and Sam has already done all the legwork. It's a no-brainer."

"Is it?" I said. I was beginning to feel pressure.

It didn't help that the kids started screaming when they heard their cousins mentioned. Oh crap, this conversation was quickly spinning out of control.

Undeterred by my obvious uncertainty, my man of action took to the Internet to further explore every bit of information Sam had provided. He was honestly so excited about the idea, I didn't have the heart to slow him down. I figured he'd roll with it for a while, and eventually the plan would fall apart. I mean, what were the chances my entire family would want to do this and we'd all be able to coordinate schedules?

Apparently, quite good. Before I knew it, the planning process had begun and went on and on and on.

While I understood that a generous amount of time was needed to properly schedule a lengthy, multi-port trip, I was not interested in spending the next eighteen months discussing all the viable options over and over again. Flight times, a hotel in Rome, cabin sizes, dinner seatings, excursions, tour guide companies, and currency exchange all had to be determined, and Tony was not at all opposed to talking through each item ad nauseam.

"Check out these two great tours," he'd say. "One has us going by car to the Colosseum, then the Pantheon, then the Vatican; the other has us going by bus to the Trevi Fountain, then the Pantheon, and ending at the Colosseum. The Vatican would be the next day. Which sounds better?"

The intensity of his conviction matched the intensity of his tone, which grew with each sentence he spoke.

"Hey, are you listening?" he admonished. "We also have to get all of our passports updated, don't forget!"

"Something tells me there's very little chance of me forgetting." I was beginning to shut down.

The planning and sharing of information continued, with detailed spreadsheets listing activities, locations, costs, and gratuities. Envelopes were distributed to each family member that included every possible bit of information one might ever need when traveling to a foreign land. Money pouches, intended to be worn under your clothing to protect against pickpockets, were included in each person's packet. Ally wasted no time bedazzling her pouch.

"Mom," she said, "Dad gave me this bag and said I have to wear it on vacation. There is no way I'm doing that because it's so ugly. So, I'm going to add some sparkle, okay?"

Man, I love that kid. She knows what she wants and never hesitates to go for it.

"You know it's supposed to be worn under your clothes, right?" I said.

"Yeah, I know, but still," she answered.

There was so much going on, it was all I could do not to run and hide in a fit of frustration. I tend to get argumentative and cranky when bogged down with too much information. I had to zip my lip, smile, and keep repeating, "That sounds great." Anyone who knows me knows that keeping my mouth shut does not come easily.

Although I couldn't be there for Tony as a fellow travel enthusiast, he was able to find support throughout the planning process in most every other adult going on the trip. I was happy that the rest of my family could share in his excitement and desire to work out the smallest of details.

The random but frequent planning conversations between Tony, my mother, and my sister were like their own little sideshows. I loved secretly listening to the banter and felt that among the three of them, and periodically my brother-in-law, they had considered and prepared for all contingencies. At a birthday celebration for Julia four months prior to our go-date, the "planning committee" was particularly vocal and engaged. I, on the other hand, was uncharacteristically silent.

"Beth, aren't you excited about this trip?" my father asked. "I'm surprised you never have anything to say about it."

"Of course, I'm excited. I just haven't given it much thought yet."

"Really? It's coming up quick. It's not like you to be so quiet. You're usually such a bigmouth."

I ignored the dig. "The truth is, the more I talk about it, the more nervous I become about getting there," I said.

"Why, the plane? Oh, come on," Dad said. "Get over it. You'll be with everyone that matters. If the plane goes down, we'll all go together."

"Oh my God, Dad, why do you say things like that?"

If only he knew how disturbing that was to me.

He, of course, had no idea and laughed at his own joke, which I didn't find funny at all. Rather than wallow, I laughed along with him, shaking my head in amused disapproval. As much as he walks the line between having a little fun and being slightly merciless, I don't mind when I'm on the receiving end of his remarks. I can take it and I respect his brand of humor. He never makes any bones about niggling a person right where it hurts. It's part of his charm.

My father is a retired teacher who continues to teach English as a second language at night. He does this partly to keep busy and partly because he's good at what he does. He's always had a way of commanding his classroom—demanding respect, yet engaging his students in a humorous way. His students and people in general naturally gravitate toward him. Dad has been able to dig up the dirtiest gossip just by asking someone how they are doing.

Like many older Greek men, Dad has a strong personality, but he is lovable. We are, in fact, a lot alike. When I was a teenager, we'd fight relentlessly until one of us gave up on the last word. One of the things that makes us different is my dad doesn't seem to worry about anything. My tendency to worry I got from my mother.

My sweet mom is a tireless and selfless supporter of our family. She managed to be the best kind of mom to my sister and me: stern, yet caring and always there for us. She raised two girls, put up with my dad, who is always a loving handful, and tolerated all the family dogs that she never wanted. Meanwhile, she took immense pride in her full-time job. She was a high-level executive assistant to several top dogs at Wang Laboratories, including Dr. An Wang himself.

Wang was a well-known computer company in the 1980s. When my sister and I were teens and Mom worked ten to twelve-hour days, we thought nothing of coming home from school, getting into an argument, and calling our mother to act as referee. We'd each grab a receiver on one of our two house phones and scream like idiots to make our points. I am sure she had no idea what we were saying, yet she never once hung up. Even though she was sitting right outside the office door of some multi-millionaire, my sister and I always knew that we came first.

And now that we were planning to go, all together, on this trip, I knew Mom couldn't have been happier. She was nearly as excited as Tony.

Finally recovering from my dad's insensitive plane comment, I said, "Dad, even if I wanted to add something, it's pointless to try to get involved. It's not like I could ever get a word in edgewise."

"Yeah, good point," he said. "I'm not getting involved either, they're nuts."

My father, Jim, or as he recently decided to refer to himself, Dimitri, is one hundred percent Greek. He is of medium height with a shock of white hair. He has worn a mustache for as long as I can remember, and the one time he shaved it, I hated it. His hair and mustache define him.

My mother, Ginny (Virginia), lovingly referred to as "Bunny" by her family, is one hundred percent Italian. She was dubbed Bunny when she was a baby because she was fair-haired, fair-skinned, petite, and cute. She's still all those things today. Her ancestors are from Fano, Italy, which is in the northern part of the country. She is the yin to my father's yang. She is calm and reserved while he is, well, not.

I was raised in the Greek Orthodox faith, so for the longest time I associated more strongly with my Greek side. I have clear memories of Sunday school at the ornate, incense-filled Transfiguration Greek Orthodox Church in Lowell, Massachusetts, and of spirited family gatherings. More than anything else, Greek food tends to be top of mind when I reminisce about my heritage. Stuffing myself with spanakopita (spinach and feta pie) and dolmades (stuffed grape leaves) were like chips at a barbecue.

And then there were those traditions I associate with my Greek grandmother. I'm not so sure they had anything to do with being Greek, other than the fact that the Greeks aren't afraid to take some food risks if it means eating something yummy.

Take one of my Yia Yia's specialties that my sister and I and our four cousins still discuss and dream about: when my Yia Yia really wanted to indulge her grandchildren, she would whip up a batch of what she called "krupo." That's not an actual word and I have no idea if that's how it should be spelled, but in our family, everyone knows what krupo is. We think the name came from the sound the mixture would make when my grandmother would feverishly stir the combination of raw egg yolks and sugar. Yes, that was it—probably about a half cup of sugar to one raw egg yolk, stirred so aggressively that the color would change from a buttery yellow to a frothy white.

Yia Yia would do the whipping and the kids would add the sugar, little by little. "More!" Yia Yia would call every time she was ready to blend more sugar. "More!" Once the consistency was just right, Yia Yia would give each grandchild a few scoops in a tea cup, and we would eat it by the spoonful, lapping up every sugary bite. Let the record show that none of us grandchildren ever suffered any ill effects from eating krupo.

Not to be outshined, my Italian side also left a marked impression. It may not come as a surprise that many of these memories also involved delicious food. One of what I'd call my truly Italian moments came when my mother took my sister and me to see her Aunt Gina and Cousin Bruna. They lived in a two story, double-decker home in East Boston and, as a child, I found the tight quarters of urban living to be alluring. I loved going into the city and felt like our visits were more like field trips than social calls. We were there to watch these two adorably authentic Italian ladies make gnocchi or prepare handpicked periwinkles (small snails) from scratch. Dough and flour were everywhere, and live periwinkles crawled about.

I could describe the experience with a fancy word, but from a kid's vantage point, it was just cool. In stereotypical Italian fashion, sweet Aunt Gina would motion to us with her hands to explain what she was doing. Had she not done us this courtesy, we would have had no idea what she was saying because of her thick Italian accent. We didn't visit often, but when we did, it was a treat.

Large holiday gatherings at Cousin Phyllis Ann's were another fond memory. Yet again food played a consequential role, especially the most amazing stuffed artichokes prepared by my mother's Aunt Bea.

"Mom, are we going to Italian Thanksgiving this year?" my sister and I would ask.

"Yes, but we are only going for dessert."

"Oh," we answered her solemnly.

"Don't worry, girls," Mom said, knowing exactly what we were thinking. "Cousin Phyllis promised to set an artichoke aside for each of you."

And she always did. As other relatives gathered to eat cannoli, ricotta pie, and Italian cookies, my sister I would happily nibble away at our artichokes, being sure to clean every last leaf of their yummy breading and tender flesh.

Food was not the only thing that stood out as truly Italian when I was with my Italian relatives. Their old school Italian names were classic and gave me the sense that I was part of the real deal. They reminded me of character names from a movie that I would happily watch over and over.

There were my grandparents, Tony (Gaetano) and Tina, the aforementioned Bruna and Gina and numerous aunts and uncles; Connie (Concetta), Al (Angelo), Jimmy (Vincenzo), Arthur, Philomena, and Rose, to name a few.

Whether I was leaning more to my Greek side or my Italian side, I've always felt like a true product of the Mediterranean. My strong roots made the anticipation of seeing where it all began even greater.

Greece and Italy are within an arm's reach. As vacation planning carried on all around me, the excitement and tension mounted. I was on a roller-coaster of emotion. In one moment I'd lose myself and get caught up thinking about the beautiful countries we'd be traveling to and how nice it would be to see them for the first time. Then, I'd snap back to reality and experience a wave of anxiety that would consume me for far longer periods of time than my fleeting moments of excitement.

Trip planning had been moving along at a steady pace for sixteen months, and I remained above the fray almost the entire time. My planning boycott saved me from overthinking the entire expedition and delayed the travel fear that I knew would eventually overcome me. When a pesky bee buzzed around my head and I squealed unnecessarily, my mother always said, "Beth, if you ignore it, it will go away." It always worked with the bees, but travel anxiety doesn't respond as well to its dismissive prey. Minor panic was creeping in.

3. The Art of Distraction

I HAD BECOME SURPRISINGLY GOOD AT SUPPRESS-
ing my nerves about the impending flight. But, as the do-
or-die moment approached, my fears became increasingly
difficult to ignore. Do or die may sound dramatic, but I saw
the flight as that. We were either going to do this thing and
be fine . . . or die. There really was no in between for me at
that time. I suspect others with flying phobias, or any other
phobia, for that matter, understand the severity of emotion
and delusion when dealing with something like this. If you've
never experienced irrational fear, I can only tell you that it
can be paralyzing in a very tangible way.

Everything I did leading up to take-off was, in one way or
another, a feeble attempt to divert my attention away from
the inevitable flight.

We were about a month away from saying "so long" to
the comforts and safety of home when I finally began giving serious thought to packing. Generally, I find packing
overwhelming. I'm always worried that I'll forget something
important, like the one and only hair gel that tames my curly
mane or my extra contact lenses if one tears. Having to walk
around Europe in my ugly old glasses would be a nightmare.

Weather is also a trouble spot. Sure, I can look ahead to
the forecast, but who trusts that? I find myself packing lots

of unnecessary alternatives in the event the climate conditions shift unexpectedly. And of course, I wondered, what's fashionable in Europe? Will my boring clothes suit Europe's superior sense of style? There were a lot of unknowns swirling around in my head, and fourteen days' worth of daytime and evening clothes would take some serious forethought and organization.

Packing for myself was one thing. Tack on Julia and Ally, and I was in for a challenge.

Thank God Tony isn't a husband who needs his wife to pack for him. That would have put me over the edge.

Rather than procrastinate, which I'm known to do, I approached this as a mission. I was focused and determined to make this the ultimate packing experience with no article of clothing, toiletry, or shoe left behind.

It was the perfect diversion. In fact, the mission became more like an obsession. There was a lot to do, and the fact that this was happening at the very end of the school year only added to the pandemonium.

We were leaving three days after the last day of school. Any parent of school-age children knows that the last couple of weeks of school are a total fiasco. Everyone is running around trying to attend end-of-year parties, buying teacher gifts, and carting children around from one field trip to another. These obligations alone make for a frantic push at the end of June. The preparations for the trip turned the entire month into a ridiculous whirlwind of activity.

When it was over, I felt frazzled with an underlying sense of triumph. I did it! I managed to get through the year-end madness and complete all my vacation shopping, packing, and primping.

The entire busy process was so therapeutic that I found myself searching for even more nonsensical things to do. When I steam-ironed every last article of clothing before placing it in its appropriate case, I knew I was in deep. I dedicated nearly a full day to this chore, which turned out to be the ultimate distraction and a clear sign that I would have done absolutely anything to avoid thinking about the plane.

"What in the heck are you doing?" Tony asked, walking in on me mid-steam. "And what is that contraption?"

"Oh, this? It's a professional grade steam machine—it's unbelievable!"

"Really? You know the minute you open your suitcase, everything in there is going to be as wrinkled as when you started," Tony said, and then added, "By the way, how much did that thing cost?"

I ignored the cost question and addressed only his cynicism regarding my new favorite household appliance. "No way, this thing has taken out so many wrinkles already; I guarantee this is time well spent. In more ways than one—trust me."

Tony didn't know what I was talking about. He thought this was all about wrinkle-free clothes.

My newly purchased, human-sized steam valet made such an impression that Karla, my sister, became as obsessed with it as I was.

Karla is my only sibling. She is two and half years older, and while we are very different, we are also very much alike. When we were young, some people thought we were twins, although her curly hair is softer and lighter than mine. Texture and color aside, our curly hair is our signature feature and makes us unmistakable as sisters. Those who know us well, however, know that Karla looks like our mother, while I look more like our dad. Karla is book smart and tight-lipped when it comes to personal matters. I'm more socially driven and am quite free with information that probably should be kept to myself. I guess that's why my dad calls me a bigmouth. Karla and I are most similar in our dry, sarcastic sense of humor and our shared desire to laugh at the most ridiculous things, including ourselves. We have a strong sisterly bond.

Karla is married to Bob, and together they have two children, Alex and Katherine. Bob is a jovial guy with a heart of gold. I always like to remind Karla that I was the one who introduced her to Bob except, of course, when she's ticked off at him, at which point I don't dare mention that fact. He is tall with sandy brown hair and is built like a linebacker. He is honestly one of the nicest guys I know, and I am not a lover of all people, so I think that says a lot. I think Bob's go-with-the-flow, happy-go-lucky approach to life is the perfect balance to my sister's more intense personality traits.

Bob and Tony were coworkers at the time we all met. It's their long-standing friendship that makes family trips, like the one we were about to take, work so well. While we all like to hang out together, Bob and Tony would much prefer to be watching a football game or playing poker, while Karla's and my idea of fun takes on a different tone.

On the day I performed my marathon steam iron session, for example, Karla joined me, and we had more fun talking and steaming than we ever could have had at a stinky bar. Without even one glass of wine, we found ourselves giddy as we steamed and commented on the state of daytime television, which played in the background. Karla was less interested in the small screen and hyper-focused on my steamer.

"This thing is unbelievable. It's so quick and easy. Nearly every wrinkle is gone. I've got to get one of these right away." Karla has the tendency to talk about things she loves as though she's a hired spokesperson. She's an advertiser's dream.

As soon as we returned home from our trip, she ran out to the store to buy her very own supersized steam iron. She, too, is now hooked on her own Steamy McSteamer.

The day after my epic ironing session, there was nothing else to do. I was officially ready to leave my house and embark on a glorious vacation. I should have been happy, but I was visibly uneasy.

"You know that, statistically speaking, it's actually safer to fly than to drive," Tony said.

"Oh my God, why do people keep telling me that?" I snapped. I'd heard it a million times already, and not one of those times did it make me feel any better.

"I just don't understand why you let yourself get so worked up. Everything is going to be fine."

I had given some thought as to why this fear had gotten so out of control and, oddly, realized it was my moderately controlling personality that might have something to do with it. Following a short bout of self-analysis, it became clear that my lack of influence over the final outcome of the flight seemed to be at the core of my phobia. I'm not physically capable of flying, so I'm as good as useless if the plane goes down. This, to me, is excruciating.

Even though the chance of getting in a car accident is much greater, when I'm driving I know it's my two hands on the wheel and my foot on the pedal. In my mind, I'm in control.

I have been asked if I also fear traveling by boat. Just months before our cruise, an Italian cruise ship capsized off the island of Giglio. It was all over the news, and the disaster resulted in thirty-two fatalities. Surprisingly, my faith in boat safety remained unchanged by this event.

"Let me get this straight," said my friend Deb. "You're afraid to fly, but you're okay with getting on a massive ship and traveling thousands of miles across the ocean with no land in sight?"

"Yeah," I answered. "I know how to swim—I could save myself if I had to."

My friend stared at me, looking vexed.

I knew it was crazy, but it made sense to me, and the last thing I needed was something else to worry about. If only I could cruise from America to Italy.

Following the last "school's out for the summer" party and one glass of wine too many, the meltdown began.

I was convinced that something awful was going to happen on that plane and that somehow, I was single-handedly putting my entire family at risk. Poor Tony had to listen to me moan and whimper until I was completely drained of tears, worries, and uncertainties.

The next day, the moment arrived. We were in Boston getting on a plane to fly eight hours to Rome's Leonardo da Vinci–Fiumicino Airport. I was stressed, excited, anxious, and glad to finally be doing it and not just thinking about it. Tony included ample buffer time to our travel schedule. His motto is, "You can never be early enough when it comes to air travel."

Inside Logan Airport, bags were checked and security cleared without delay. We had about two hours to kill before our flight at five-ten p.m. My parents were with us. Karla and her family had flown out two days prior, so they could spend more time in Rome.

I really could've used my sister's chatter to distract me. Instead, I decided to make effective use of the time and sought out a little liquid courage. A quick gin and tonic, a vodka martini, a glass of wine—really anything along these lines would help to dull the senses. I was not alone. Tony and my dad happily joined me in a calming cocktail while my mom and the girls enjoyed something on the softer side.

I was quiet and disengaged from conversation. I questioned whether I should have followed the advice my sister had given me a couple of weeks prior. Karla struggled with her own fear of flying. But in the weeks leading up to departure, I noticed she wasn't nervous at all.

"I'm so stressed out about flying," I said to her. "How is it that you're so relaxed? I thought you hated flying."

"I still do, but I've managed to get it under control over the past few years."

"Okay, don't leave me hanging! What are you doing? I'm freaking out over here!"

"Relax! It's not like I go around publicizing it, so don't go telling everybody."

"Really? Who the hell am I going to tell? Just tell me already."

"All right, a little Lorazepam does the trick," she said. "Just enough to stay calm and get a little sleep."

It certainly sounded like a reasonable solution, and I'm sure that any kind of happy pill would have been better than nothing. But I hesitated, as I pictured myself having an adverse reaction to the mood-altering drug and then morphing into a raving lunatic.

"Just try one in advance to see how you respond," Karla said.

"Right, okay, I'll think about it."

I didn't think about it and I didn't do it. I don't even take NyQuil, for God's sake.

I may not be adventurous with pills, but I have never been shy with a cocktail. Back at the airport lounge, it was somewhere between three-thirty and four p.m. I'm not much of a day drinker, but desperate times. . . . I decided on wine. Not too strong, but just enough to take the edge off. Two glasses of a nice, full-bodied red, and I always drift off to sleep at the first hum of a car's engine. Why would this occasion be different than any other?

"Are you really going to drink a glass of wine now?" my mother questioned.

"Actually, no, I'm having two."

"Hmph," said Mom with a raised eyebrow and a disapproving glare.

I should have gone with something much stronger.

By the time I boarded, I had reached a state of acceptance. This was happening and there was no point panicking now. As anyone might expect when traveling in coach, it was long and uncomfortable, and never for a moment did I escape the nagging feeling that every little bump or blip would result in the plane plummeting to earth to our inevitable demise.

The first few hours were fine. I fed off the kids' excitement and remained focused on listening to their enthusiasm. I knew that eventually everyone would sleep, and I wanted nothing more than to do the same. By nine p.m., my seat had become increasingly uncomfortable, and the little kid directly behind me became restless. As other passengers began turning off overhead lights, primping pillows and pulling up blankets, I grew less and less sleepy and more and more irritable.

The little girl behind me proceeded to kick and push the back of my chair at intermittent intervals for hours. There was a moment of reprieve when the kicking stopped. Finally, I thought I might doze off, but no—the little girl replaced her penchant for kicking with an even more annoying light show. With my armrest in the upright position, the troublesome toddler had full access to my light controls and took full advantage. It took me several minutes to realize that it was her. I snatched my armrest back down by my side with a snarl and a stare that resulted in even more annoying giggling.

It seemed like the little girl and I were the only passengers still awake. By this time, it must have been at least midnight back home. I had no idea what time zones we'd crossed over yet. However, I did know that if I didn't catch some Z's soon, I'd be in big trouble come our European morning. We would arrive in Rome a little after one a.m. Eastern Standard Time, seven a.m. Central European Time. The plan was to come off the plane with enough rest to be ready for a new day in Rome, chock-full of things to do from beginning to end. The more I worried about sleeping, the more I couldn't. Inside the airplane, all else was still and quiet. It was weird. I really wished the wine had done its job.

4. Rome

WE MADE IT. WITH BOTH FEET SET FIRMLY ON THE
ground, I let out a long breath. I was so ridiculously glad
that the flight was over. Although weary from the ride, the
build up from months of planning, anticipation, and anxiety
fueled us with punchy enthusiasm. I was genuinely excited
to begin exploring the first of our three major destinations
in Europe, and from the energized expressions on everyone
else's faces, they were, too. Tony stepped right to it and effi-
ciently directed us to our shuttle service to the hotel.

"Listen up, everybody," he commanded. "Let's move
quickly to baggage claim. I don't want to get stuck behind a
crowd of slowpokes. Follow me and stay close."

He navigated his way through the airport at lightning
speed, never once taking into consideration that his tall person legs were moving much faster than any of us could keep
up with.

"Would you slow down, please?" I said, knowing full well
my request would fall on deaf ears.

Despite the unnecessary scurry, we managed to make it to
baggage claim together, at which point the kids caught their
breath, and a series of typical kid questions followed.

"Dad, how long will it take to get to the hotel?"

"Can we go swimming right when we get there?"

"How soon after we get to the hotel are we leaving again?"

"When will we see Alex and Katherine?"

Another bonus to having not participated in the planning was that the kids eventually realized I was not a reliable source of information, so they stopped hounding me with questions after the first two or three times I told them I didn't know.

There really was no time to waste as we made our way to Rome's Crowne Plaza–St. Peter's Hotel, just outside the heart of the city. We went straight from the airport, unloaded our bags at the hotel, and waited for my sister and her family to meet us there. Our first sightseeing expedition was scheduled at two-thirty p.m. This was why sleeping on the plane would've been nice. I hoped the six-hour time difference and lack of sleep would not catch up with me.

The hotel was lovely, if not a bit typical. Patterned carpeting, neutral toned walls, and basic contemporary styling defined the space as we first entered. I was not overcome with a sense of European flair, but I was happy to be in a place that was clean, comfortable, and stylish. Dad took this brief opportunity to lay down (smart man) while the rest of us settled in, each in our own way. The girls were trying to figure out the TV, my mom was puttering around her room answering to my father's every beck and call. Unfortunately for her, my dad got enough sleep on the plane that he had just enough energy to call out commands while fully tucked into his hotel bed. That man is nothing if not spoiled. I collapsed on a bed. This was the perfect time to sneak in a quick nap, but I've never been able to sleep in daylight hours. Instead,

I lay there motionless and tried to collect myself. And then there was Tony.

"Oh, please tell me you aren't actually unpacking your bag," I said to him.

"I am—you know, just the things I need while we're here."

"It's only two days; can't you just live out of your bag for that long?"

"Are you seriously questioning me unpacking after your insane packing ordeal at home?"

The Kittlers arrived to jumps of joy from Julia and Ally, and once pleasantries had been exchanged, we began the process of gathering everyone together to head out for our first tour.

The gaggle of us rallied our way out of the hotel to meet our tour guide. As Tony and Bob asked for directions, the rest of us sat on a curb awaiting the thumbs up to move forward. I looked back at my family members' red faces and slumped shoulders and realized how hot it was. We were prepared, hydrated, and appropriately dressed in comfortable shorts and sleeveless tops, but man, there was no denying the soul-sucking power of such a hot day—this by our New England summer standards, anyway. The good news was that it wasn't humid like we are all too familiar with back home. But the temperature had to have been in the mid-nineties, and we felt it with every ounce of our travel-fatigued bodies. Like getting a bit too close to a fire, you could feel the heat on your skin and those of us who sweat a lot (Tony) were already dripping.

We had only just exited the hotel. As we got moving and our body temperatures rose even further, I knew the dominating heat would take some getting used to. This aside, my first glimpses of Rome drew me in and helped me forget the weather-related discomfort. I understood right away why Karla and Bob had wanted to spend some extra time here.

Rome is a fabulous city that rivals the busy energy of Manhattan, but with an Old-World elegance and atmosphere that one might expect of a city founded in 753 B.C. It wasn't the phenomenal architecture alone that stood out as we made our way into the heart of the city, but there seemed to be an overall sense of style and sophistication throughout the crowds of people we saw that I found completely captivating. I felt like I had arrived at the land of the pretty people. I was surrounded by beauty and loved the feeling that I was some-place special. My immediate sense that Rome was a place of perfection and high standards didn't prevent it from acting as host to what turned out to be one of the funniest adventures we would experience throughout the trip.

"I like Rome," I said to Tony.

"How do you know, we've barely seen it?" Tony said.

"I know. But I remember the first time I went to New York City and I expected everyone on the street to look like a supermodel and, of course, no one did—but here, they kind of do."

When I first gave serious consideration to our Mediterra-nean travels, I rarely thought about the cities we'd be visiting. Rome and Athens were the last places on my mind. Rather, my visions were always of mountains, cliffs, fields, beaches, islands, and quaint villages. I think photos I'd seen of my sis-ter's previous trip to Tuscany left me thinking that tranquil scenes like the ones she'd shared were what I could expect.

I tend to underestimate the power of a great city. I always assume that the pace will be too fast and the crowds too plentiful. I felt the same way when I went to London and Paris, yet was pleasantly surprised by each of those cities, just as I ended up being with Rome.

The historical significance of a city like Rome and its many attractions made for a place that even the most anti-urban person could appreciate. These things, plus the effortless marriage between all things old and new, spoke to me in a big way. I found it so interesting that we'd pass by a typical series of storefronts on one street, only to turn the corner and find ourselves gazing upon an amazingly ancient-looking piece of architecture that somehow flowed perfectly and didn't look out of place whatsoever. This trend continued throughout our travels, and I remained fascinated by it the entire time.

I couldn't believe that in the brief time we'd been on the streets of Rome, making our way to our first official tour, I'd already become so engrossed in my surroundings. Any travel jitters leftover from the flight melted away with anticipation for what was to follow. Or maybe they had melted away with the unrelenting heat. Europe was hot—really hot. I was sure thermometers would break a hundred degrees by day's end and as far as I was concerned, any hundred-degree day should be spent indoors with air-conditioning cranked. Honestly, I think eighty-degree days are a bit much, and here we were spending our day outside. I knew what we were in for, but the moment I felt those first beads of sweat build on my brow and the droplets drip from my chest, I thought, oh crap—I hope this doesn't slow us down. Poor Julia was so hot that as we walked to our meeting spot for the tour, the sweat dripping from her forehead caused the sunscreen to seep into her eyes. She was bloodshot, teary-eyed, and uncomfortable all day. I felt so guilty for insisting she wear the sunscreen and hoped it would be the worst of our heat-induced issues.

Side note: If we were to go back, I would time our travel for one of Europe's cooler months.

Our first tour of Rome took us on a romp through the city on a guided golf cart tour. That's right, I said golf cart.

I was aware that this would be our mode of transportation, having heard it from Tony and Karla several times, but it wasn't until I set eyes on the little cruisers that I questioned the legitimacy of this choice. I hadn't had the forethought to envision our crew of ten motoring around the very busy streets of Rome in wide open golf carts with no seatbelts or enclosure to prevent us from injury. The moment I saw them, I blurted out, "What the hell is this? Are we really going to load all of the kids and adults onto these things?"

Tony gave me a curt look, which was my cue to zip it. But I couldn't help but be concerned.

"Mom, come on, you can't possibly be comfortable with this?" I asked in a hushed voice, knowing if I were to get support on this, it would be from my mother. We both surveyed the line of pseudo-vehicles with critical glares.

"Hmmm, I don't know," she said. "I'm sure that when Tony arranged this he ensured they'd be fine, but I do agree that they seem a little unsafe."

I grumbled with aggravation, knowing my mother loved Tony too much to ever question his judgment. I swear both my parents have a softer spot for Tony than they do for me.

Safe or not, I would soon find out that we were in for a hilarious, wild ride that was also surprisingly informative.

There were three carts between the Kittler, Thomas, and Daigle crew, and one other cart for some other tour goers. I'm guessing they wished they'd chosen another tour that wasn't monopolized by a rowdy group of ten. Everyone wore headphones tuned into the lead guide's microphone. It was odd at first, but I wasn't driving, so really all I had to do was listen and look.

Finn was our guide for the day. He had come to Rome from Ireland as a student. He had attended the University of Rome and decided to stay on following graduation because he, like so many others, had fallen in love with the city.

He was tall with blond, wavy hair and a cheery smile and attitude. Most importantly, he was well-informed and comfortable teaching while driving. Tony and Bob drove two of the carts for our group, my parents and Karla rode with Finn. It was surprising that this touring company put so much faith in foreign drivers who were likely unfamiliar with European automobile travel. Regardless, all drivers passed whatever test was required to take position behind the steering wheel, and off we went.

The delightful atmosphere around Rome immediately put me at ease. I found myself focusing on the modern buildings and storefronts that were familiar in style and purpose to what I knew at home. There were typical-looking convenience stores, lunch spots, and clothing boutiques. Their sleek, modern construction and inviting window displays reminded me of many an urban retail district that I'd strolled down in the past.

Before long, we'd rolled out of the new section of the city and abruptly found ourselves bumping alongside streets paved in stone. Golf carts are clearly not made for this type of terrain. Building facades had quickly gone from expected to spectacular, and it finally hit me that indeed I was in Italy. I wanted to take it all in, and I began with a deep breath. The urban air smelled good, not heavy as I've come to expect from major cities like New York or Los Angeles. Although I couldn't see any eateries from where I sat in my golf cart, I was sure one was nearby, as a faint hint of yeasty dough lingered in the air. Authentic pizza must not have been far either. I couldn't wait to experience it.

The buildings that I was now looking at were dramatic and detailed. The intricate designs and patterns on their facades were a vast contrast from what we'd observed just one street over. The sidewalks were busy with people, but not crowded. There was good energy around us, but not so much that I felt overwhelmed or intimidated. In fact, it was rather inviting. So much so that I couldn't wait to hop out of the golf cart and get closer to the action.

The people here seemed different than what I was used to at home, too, but in a good way. The men and women on the streets walked at a leisurely pace and were well dressed. Many of the women were in heels. Not stilettos, but heels thin and high enough that I would think walking on these uneven streets would be a bit treacherous. They wore flowing skirts, pretty tops, and seemed unaffected by the heat.

Men wore loose-fitting dress shirts, rolled at the sleeves, slacks, and dress shoes. I envisioned them meeting the lovely ladies in the flowing skirts for a nice dinner.

More than their clothes, the thing that struck me most about the people I saw were the expressions on their faces. They did not appear stressed; their heads were up, and they made eye contact with one another. Some smiled, some waved hello, and some just strode along in what appeared to be a peaceful state. They were not rushed, and they held themselves in a way that made it seem they were content in what they were doing and where they were going.

I found myself envying this "live in the moment" manner that permeated the atmosphere. The pride each person took in their outward appearance was also something that lit a spark in me. I wanted to be like that and to feel like that. I had a lot to learn from this lifestyle.

"Is it just me, or does everyone look so nice here?" I said to Tony.

"No, I've actually noticed it, too. They do look sharp. It's nice."

"I wish we could look like this more often at home."

"Why can't we?"

"Come on," I said. "Are you really going to give up your cargo shorts and ratty T-shirt to run errands on the weekends?"

"Run errands? Why would I get dressed up for errands?"

That was my point. Unless Tony's going to the office or we have a special occasion, we find ourselves looking sloppy in jeans, sweatshirts or, my personal favorite, yoga pants. This is how people see us out and about town on a regular basis. Our dress-down culture is certainly comfortable, but after being in Italy for just a short time, I began thinking it was really time to step up our day-to-day fashion.

While for the most part, I'm content with my American suburban life, I was hopelessly intrigued with what I perceived to be the ease of European living and the dignity apparent in the folks who took the time to present themselves in a respectable, put-together manner. It was almost absurd to think that I could've picked up on this "enviable" lifestyle from the vantage point of my golf cart. Not to mention the short time we'd been on foreign ground, but I knew something was different here, and it felt good. It was hard to believe that less than twelve hours prior, I was a basket case in an airport.

When I thought about life at home, I struggled with what I knew to be the typical American hustle and bustle of absolutely everything. People are much too eager to brag about how busy or important they are. "I've been running around all day getting Jimmy to football and Emily to gymnastics and I've got three more loads of laundry to do before I get dinner on the table," or "I've been in back-to-back meetings all day and still managed to make a million dollars for my client." Yeah, yeah, we all get it because we're all doing the same thing in one way or another. There's no need to brag or compete about it, because honestly, it's not all that impressive and we, as a society, desperately need to slow down. Getting away from that had brought about an immediate sense of calm.

I found myself fixating on the folks gathered leisurely on stoops—some sitting, some standing. Some were chatting and drinking coffee while others were smoking. Couples walked slowly, hand in hand, and I couldn't help but notice that not one of these locals had any sense of urgency for whatever was coming next in their day. Not once did I see that harried scowl and furrowed brow that I so often see on the faces of people at home. I was convinced that the Italian people were on to something that we, as Americans, were missing.

That is, until we ventured away from the sidewalks and braved the streets by golf cart. Suddenly an entirely different kind of Italian energy emerged. It was like hell on wheels all around us. Cars were darting in and out, and drivers hollered aggressively at one another. Meanwhile, pedestrians never once adjusted their gait as vehicles raced toward them. I'm sure they were used to the chaos, or maybe they knew that one slight change of pace could result in their heel being clipped by the tires of the frenetic driver.

"*Spostare, spostare* [move, move]!" one driver shouted.

"*Stai zitto* [shut up]!" another yelled back.

Meanwhile, motorcyclists were everywhere, wildly moving at race car speeds. Men in fancy slacks and lovely ladies in skirts and heels scooted about on their Vespas as if in a mad rush to get somewhere very important. Dressed to the nines or not, it seemed that whatever aggression these otherwise easygoing Italians had built up inside of them was completely released when they hopped in the driver's seat.

I couldn't believe the drastic contrast between the composed personalities we witnessed walking along the city streets to the frenzy on the road.

If watching the speedy drivers wasn't enough, being a passenger on a golf cart in the middle of all of it really had me worried.

At one point along the tour, I was positioned on the back seat of the cart facing oncoming traffic. This didn't faze me, as I don't experience motion sickness.

"You don't mind riding backwards, do you, Beth?" Tony asked.

"No, I don't care. It's fine."

My only previous experience with golf carts had been in the little lake house community of New Hampshire where Tony and I owned a summer home. There, golf cart travel is permitted on the quiet, private roads leading up to the beach. Travel on public roads with these mobile contraptions is strictly prohibited.

This law obviously doesn't hold up in Italy, because our little tour took us onto all sorts of major roads with the crazy fast Italian drivers hustling all around us.

Hanging off the back of our cart, I held on for dear life as we attempted to keep pace with traffic and simultaneously not lose our caravan. It wasn't until I was faced with one particularly anxious bus driver that I began to worry that we might not end our excursion with the same number of people as we began. As traffic slowed and my cart came to a near stop, the bus pulled up behind me so closely and so quickly I could've leaned over and kissed it.

As the bus approached, I didn't know what else to do other than to squeal in horror and cover my eyes—I was sure I was about to meet my fate. It all happened so quickly that I froze, unable to think of a better way to save myself and others on board.

"What is going on back there—why are you screaming?" Tony shouted.

"I'm about to be flattened by a bus!"

When Tony looked back to see how close the bus really had come, all he could say was, "Holy crap!"

After this ride, I concluded that golf carts need to stay right where they belong—on the golf course.

Transportation aside, our tour on wheels allowed us to see many special places in Rome. Many more than we would have had we been on foot or even bus. Among the major sights were the Pantheon, the Colosseum, and the Vatican. These were our must-see places. Not to see them would be like visiting Paris without seeing the Eiffel Tower. We only drove past the Colosseum and Vatican, but our visit inside the Pantheon gave me my first taste of the grandeur of Roman architecture.

The Pantheon

Built around 120 AD, the Pantheon is a magnificently preserved ancient temple located in the busy Piazza della Rotonda. From the exterior, it is surrounded by more modern-day buildings. To walk through it is a feast for the eyes. Geometric shapes from floor to ceiling occupy the space. Grand fluted columns with elaborate moldings draw your eye upward toward the dome, which reaches a maximum height of nearly one hundred and forty-two feet. The oculus, eye of the Pantheon, the circular opening at the center of the dome, allows visitors to see up and out to the gods above.

Pantheon means "honor all gods." The oculus is the only source of natural light in the building. Otherwise, when inside, you are completely enclosed. The sense of containment and separation from the outside world offered a safe and spiritual feeling in which I was pleasantly lost for several undistracted moments. If my pinched neck hadn't begged for relief, I may have continued to peer through the oculus's window to heaven much longer. Lifelike statues surround you and are individually housed in their own distinct alcoves. As you walk the perimeter of the circular room, you can't help but revere them as is intended. Tombs and art occupy more of the space. The church altar is understated, yet maintains a powerful draw. The Pantheon continues to operate as a church. I imagine the sacred connection during one of these church services to be unsurpassed. I said a quick prayer because it almost seemed a sacrilege not to. I thanked God for getting us to this most beautiful place safely and prayed for continued enlightenment.

5. Off the Beaten Path

I LOVE BEING DIFFERENT AND DOING DIFFERENT things. I have nothing against the norm, but for as long as I can remember, I've always wanted to take a personalized approach to almost everything.

Back in middle school, when most girls looked to blend in and follow the latest fads, I often chose to do my own thing. To some degree, my uniqueness was out of my control. I was a feisty, Greek girl in a school full of proper, Catholic young ladies, and while most of my classmates donned pin straight bobs, I had a mass of crazy, curly locks. Being Greek and having curly hair set me apart in what I considered to be a good way. I was lucky as a kid that being different fueled me rather than troubled me. Now I realize I'm actually wired in such a way that I thrive on eccentricity. The older I get, the more I crave the unusual or unexpected.

This tendency was true even when traveling through Europe. Of course, I loved seeing the big attractions, but I found myself more drawn to the places I knew less about.

Having an adventurous tour guide was particularly helpful in this regard. If left to sight-see Rome on our own, I suspect we would have stuck to the major sights. I highly doubt we'd have been daring enough to take our large crowd to lesser-known locations. Finn, however, exposed us to several spots in Rome that we would not have discovered on our own.

Monumento Nazionale a Vittorio Emanuele II

The National Monument of Victor Emmanuel II in Rome's Piazza Venezia was one of them. I had never heard of it, but was wowed by it the minute it came into view. It stands between the Capitoline Hill and Piazza Venezia and struck me as an elaborate combination of a medieval castle, with a touch of the White House, topped off with a nod to the Parthenon. All of this merged together into one standout piece of architecture.

Constructed of stark white marble, this building was made to honor the first king of a united Italy. Victor Emmanuel II must have been quite a guy, because the exterior of this building alone had everything from a grand staircase to towers and columns galore. It was prominent and radically set apart from its more ordinary surroundings.

It is nicknamed the "wedding cake" by the Italian people, I suppose because of the facade's surprisingly white, frosting-like resemblance. I personally found to it be grand, but the Italians dislike it for its ostentatiousness and dissimilarity to the more patinaed structures around it.

The "wedding cake," while eye-catching, was not a scheduled stop. I was satisfied with the quick look we got while driving by, but I did not feel the same about the Colosseum.

Yes, this was a major tourist attraction, but I wanted the chance to step inside, if even for a quick look. Regrettably, we merely looped it on the street in an effort to stick to our agenda and keep up with our caravan of carts. I envied my sister and family who'd toured it in the two days they were in Europe without us, and my parents, who'd visited it in a previous trip they'd taken years ago. This was disappointing, but as Tony optimistically suggested, it was an excuse to come back another time.

We were off to our next stop, and when all the golf carts came to a stop, everyone hopped out with the same bewildered expression: Where the heck are we?

Il Buco di Roma

We had landed at one of Rome's lovely secret gardens, created centuries ago for the private pleasure of aristocrats like Napoleon Bonaparte. These hidden gems are tucked away behind stone walls and gates and can be easily missed. If you are well traveled or watch a lot of travel TV, you may be familiar with this little treasure, but it was new to us and especially the kids, who found it most intriguing.

"Don't let your first glance fool you," said Finn. "The beauty lies behind."

We had pulled up to what looked like a building's entrance, but the entrance facade was not backed by a building; rather, it was flanked by a solid wall, complete with decorative trim and designs. Everything was so large, it was impossible to make any guesses about what was behind the barrier.

"What's he talking about?" Julia said.

"I really don't know," I said. "Let's go see." Finn's cryptic statement had sparked my curiosity.

We had reached the Piazza Dei Cavalieri di Malta, or Knights of Malta. This former palace-turned-monastery-turned-base for the Sovereign Military Order of Malta, is located on Aventine Hill. Here, Il Buco di Roma or, the Hole of Rome, gives unsuspecting visitors a surprising sight. The property is home to a garden that is not open to the public. The only way for unauthorized visitors to appreciate its lush landscape is to walk directly up to the entryway's large, green wooden doors and peer through the tiny keyhole.

Through this narrow, inch-long opening we saw a painting-like panorama of elaborate green gardens. In the distance, St. Peter's Basilica was the pinnacle of the scene, set majestically on the horizon. At first peek, the eye is drawn down a tunnel of arching greenery past which rooftops and trees draw the eye back up to the highest visible point of St. Peter's picturesque dome, framed colorfully by blue skies. I couldn't take my eye off the exquisite and peaceful scene behind those doors. I would've liked to have lingered much longer, but I was swiftly shoved aside by the youngsters in our group. The idea that we were admiring something forbidden or private made it more mesmerizing. I left Il Buco di Roma with a tingling anticipation for what was to come. The next unplanned stop to capture my attention was the Torre Argentina cat sanctuary.

Torre Argentina

This unusual square was set below ground level in the middle of an otherwise busy retail district. Right there, in the midst of modern buildings and people walking and biking about, were the remains of the republican Roman temples. The existence of this bit of ruins, so oddly situated in the middle of a busy, current day square, was thought-provoking on its own. But to learn that the area was now a volunteer-run cat shelter further piqued my interest. My fifteen-year-old nephew Alex and I stood by the rails that enclosed the ruins. We quietly overlooked the shelter for a bit longer than the rest.

"What is this place, ShaSha?" asked Alex. (ShaSha is my auntie moniker given to me by Alex when he was just learning to speak. He couldn't say auntie, but always referred to me as something that sounded like *shasha*, so it stuck.)

"It's the ruins of a Roman temple," I said.

"Why is it still here?"

What a good question, I thought. Alex had always been an insightful kid.

Why were the ruins still there? Despite its seemingly dilapidated state, in a part of the city that had been newly built around it, there it remained—broken yet strong. My mind wandered as I thought about how nice it was to see a piece of history right in front of me and not just in a book. I found it commendable that the people of Europe placed such value on the worn and tattered remnants of times past. I couldn't help but think about America's obsession with real estate development and all things shiny and new. I wondered why we didn't maintain the same level of respect the Europeans have for historically significant ruins and structures. The presence of these fallen structures adds so much depth and character to the places where they exist. Their imperfection was part of the beauty.

Would similarly damaged or worn-out places in America be purchased by developers, torn down, and redesigned into modern-day condominiums?

Are we, as Americans, hasty and unsentimental? Where are the ruins of our short history? No sooner does something break or fall in America, then we rush to clean it up, erect a memorial and erase the tragedy, the mistakes, and the history of what happened there. Some might see this as advancement and forward thinking, but I wonder how much of those moments in time are lost forever. Is what was once there, while broken and damaged, wiped away too quickly, only to be a distant memory that future generations will never fully understand?

This question would come to mind repeatedly throughout our journey as ruins, historical sites, and aged monuments continued to have a profound impact on me.

I love what has been upheld and cherished in Europe as historically worthwhile, even if run down and unsightly in appearance. I suppose this is a fitting example of beauty being in the eye of the beholder. There is something sacred about these grounds, knowing that people lived and died there.

In my own hometown of Lowell, Massachusetts, mill buildings represent a large part of that city's history and culture. Some of those buildings have been torn down, and many have been turned into office space, condos, or artists' studios. These modern-day transformations are a beneficial use of the space in lieu of tearing the buildings down entirely, but I wonder what might have been retained if those mills had just been left alone. What might visitors have discovered if they could walk through the buildings as they once were? What buried artifacts might have been unearthed? The church where I was married, St. Cecilia's in Wolfeboro, New Hampshire, was renovated and turned into a music hall. It saddens me that I can never return to the place where Tony and I exchanged our vows. So many sacred churches have seen a similar fate, and in many ways, it's like memories being erased. I wish we, in America, held a little more tightly to our past.

Roaming through the ruins in the heart of Rome allowed me to transport myself to another time and truly imagine what life might have been like back when the Roman temple at the cat sanctuary was constructed.

Feeling the stones beneath my feet while attempting to piece together a full picture of a partial building that stood in front of me was one of the greatest pleasures of the trip. It would be hard to reach this same level of imaginative time travel in a restored or redesigned historical space.

I never answered Alex's question about why the sanctuary remained. I had so quickly become enamored with Rome that I was daydreaming like a teenager on a date with Italy and Rome. I had a crush.

Absolutely everything I encountered for the first three or four days looked as fabulous and glamorous to me as my very first pair of glitzy Jimmy Choos. I was very quickly forgetting any reservations I once had about this trip, and travel in general, for that matter. The transition was like jumping into cold water on a hot day. Once you're in it is wonderful, but the hesitation to take the first chilly step can be crippling.

The food, the shops, the statues, and the buildings were all extraordinary to me. Yet it was the people that were most captivating. Did the beautiful people of Europe have something that we Americans didn't? And when I say beautiful, they were all naturally beautiful. No bottle blondes with fake boobs or facelifts. These people were authentically attractive.

"Karla, am I in some kind of sleep-deprived, European trance, or is everyone here seriously good-looking?"

"I know, I've never seen anything like it. If it's something in their water, then we'd better drink up."

At one point—I swear I'm not exaggerating—we drove by a garbage truck, and when I looked up to see the driver I just blurted out loud, "Are you seeing this? Is this place for real? That guy is totally hot and he's driving a garbage truck, for God's sake." I'm sorry, but the garbage men in my neighborhood do *not* look anything like that!

I realized I was staring, but this guy was undeniably good-looking with his dark hair, dark eyes, chiseled jaw, and five o'clock shadow. Even the glint of sweat and garbage truck wheels couldn't convince me that this man wasn't attractive.

Karla craned forward to get a good look and simply said, "Oh my!"

The next thing to make a big impression was the Pasquino protests.

Pasquino Protests

Enchanting little notes were posted near or on what are known as Rome's "talking statues." There are several statues throughout the city that essentially act as outdoor bulletin boards for curious comments. The first was named Pasquino after its creator. Spirited political activists express themselves by posting handwritten messages of discontent, criticism, or commentary, often against the papacy. They were Rome's version of graffiti, but easily removed. Something about the passion and time taken to write and post these notes spoke volumes to me. No Facebook ramblings or Twitter rants, just good old paper and pen, fastened to a wall with tape.

And not too far from our talking statue sighting was the Piazza Navona.

Piazza Navona

This charming city square is home to the imposing Fontana dei Quattro Fiumi (Fountain of the Four Rivers), the intricacies of which were mind-boggling. As I approached the fountain, I couldn't help but feel small. The statues of the river gods that sit at the base are the size of giants, and the center obelisk stands over fifty feet tall. The gods each represent one of four rivers: Danube, Río de la Plata, the Nile, and the Ganges. The football-stadium length of the piazza itself added to the area's grand impression. This public gathering space was the perfect spot for our hot and tired group to catch its breath and let the day's sightseeing sink in.

Artists sat cross-legged on the ground, surrounded by their masterpieces. They worked on new creations, unaffected by those of us peering over their shoulder to watch them in action. Street performers passed by to show off their talents as well. It reminded me a bit of Faneuil Hall Marketplace in Boston.

At one point we encountered a very human-looking body seated on a chair in jeans, sneakers, a suit jacket, dress shirt, and tie. The way the legs were crossed looked real; however, this figure had no head—just a floating hat and sunglasses with no discernable wires keeping them in place. I really wanted to touch it, but I had this suspicious feeling that that would end with me looking like a fool.

In another part of the piazza, men in metallic suits and silver makeup strode by on stilts. They must have stood about eight feet tall. One of these characters drew Ally in a little too close as he attempted to shake her hand. She promptly decided this was not to her liking.

"Mom, that tall guy made me nervous," Ally told me as she came running over.

"Why? What happened?"

"He shook my hand, but I felt like he wasn't going to let go, so I yanked my hand away and took off."

Friendly Italian street performer versus stranger-danger suspicious American. My guess is that the towering character meant no harm, but we decided to stick with our skeptical American ways and keep the kids close. As fun and beautiful as these neat and new things were, we were still in unfamiliar territory.

Cafés and food vendors filled the plaza. Everything looked and smelled so tempting.

People-watching was at its highest level between the artists we'd already come across and the fellow tourists who were around us taking in the same scene. I found myself eavesdropping on accents and observing outfits to try to determine where people were from. I wondered if we, as Americans, stood out. I hoped not.

I couldn't have been happier with the simple pleasures of Rome. It felt good to feel positive about everything we were seeing and doing. No complaints, no concerns, no negatives;

we were living in the moment and loving it, especially the food.

Creamy gelato, homemade pasta, and pizza were available on nearly every corner. I think we indulged in gelato five times in our short time in Rome. It became such a go-to, refreshing snack that the Kittlers started their own gelataria competition, ruling in the end that their favorite was a place called Valentino's.

The sights on our plates rivaled the sights on the streets. And while I love to eat, I do try to balance my voracious appetite with some modicum of portion control. If I had stopped and eaten something every time I was tempted in Rome, I never would have made it through the rest of the trip. We were only just getting started, and I knew I had to pace myself.

Growing up, I was served a wide variety of wonderful foods and have come to love diverse types of cuisine. There was no chance I would come to Italy and Greece and not take full advantage of the authentic Mediterranean fare. I just had to be smart. I chose wisely, and what I did eat, I welcomed and enjoyed every morsel with no regrets or guilt.

In Italy, especially, I imagined the food would be half of the vacation experience. I was not about to miss out because, despite my broad and adaptable palate, I don't often experiment with different foods at home and don't eat out that often. I often find myself eating the same old things. It can be boring, but I can't seem to get myself out of the food rut that comes with life on the go, coupled with Tony's food allergies and two picky eaters.

In addition to being a steadfast meat and potatoes guy, Tony has one of the oddest food allergies I've ever heard of:

both chicken and turkey. Options are very limited when it comes to foods Tony can or will eat. The only tougher food critic in my house is my youngest. Ally is a typical American kid, which means she is a picky eater who eats chicken nuggets, mac 'n' cheese, and hamburgers. If it's processed and bad for you, she likes it.

I never wanted to be one of those moms who makes three different meals a night, but sadly I've fallen victim to that domestic trap. I may be a homebody, but home cooked meals are not my thing. Italy gave me a whole new respect for food—how we get it, how we prepare it, and how we eat it.

At dinner that night in a little eatery we stumbled upon near our hotel, I looked at my mom and said, "You know I love your Italian food, but the food here is really something else."

"I can't disagree," she said, and we both downed a mouthful of the tastiest pasta Bolognese.

6. The Vatican

IN THE NAME OF THE FATHER, THE SON, AND THE Holy Spirit—our second day in Rome was reserved entirely for the Vatican. I was channeling my holiest of virtues and ready to see if day two would live up to day one.

I was not alone in thinking that Rome was intoxicating.

"I love Roma," Tony announced, impetuously adopting the local lingo of *Roma* versus *Rome*. "I want to come back and stay for a month."

"Oh God," I said. "Here we go."

I couldn't begrudge his enthusiasm. I would have liked more time in this, the Eternal City. Aptly named by the Roman people who believed Rome would go on forever, just as I wished our time here would.

We had one more day before we were to depart for our ten-day Mediterranean cruise. It was hard to believe that "the trip" hadn't even officially begun.

Our time in Rome would not have been complete without a visit to the Vatican. With an entire day blocked expressly for this one destination, I knew to prepare myself physically, mentally, and fashionably.

I was ready for and open to a religious awakening. Where better for this to happen than the Vatican?

The fact that I am not Catholic did not lessen my anticipation. Although I was brought up Greek Orthodox, I attended an all-girls Catholic school for nine years, as did my sister. I knew very well what it meant to be a good Catholic. In fact, Julia and Ally were attending our local Catholic school back home, so anything I may have forgotten from my years of religious education had been recently and adequately refreshed through them.

Tony, a lifelong Catholic and former altar boy, trumped us all when it came to embracing a Catholic way of life. He was always trying to be a faithful follower, showing up to church on Sunday. Funny how he always pushed for the mass after which donuts were served. Between him and the kids being at Catholic school, I felt comfortable and well prepared for our Vatican visit.

Wrong! Once there, I quickly realized that beyond wearing clothing to conceal one's knees and shoulders, I had no clue what the Vatican experience was really about. I could not have imagined the indescribable breadth of it and was utterly impressed, if not overwhelmed.

All the buildings that comprise the Vatican, and there are many, are contained within its own independent city–state limits. Furthermore, Vatican City is its own country within the city of Rome. It is the smallest country in the world, encircled by a two-mile border. Some of the more familiar buildings include the Vatican Museum, the Apostolic Palace, St. Peter's Basilica, and the Sistine Chapel. Each one of these places could consume a full day of our time on their own, but we were on the fast track to get through all of them at once.

Small as it was, this little country, with a birth rate of zero, seemed to have no end. My impression of the main building from an exterior vantage point was that it was grand and formal. Maybe I'd been slapped on the wrist one too many times by my Catholic school's nuns, but everything about this seemed as serious and mighty as one might expect. No jokes or giggles today—I had my game face on, and I was ready to behave just as a good girl should. Now, what was I to do about the rest of my crew?

We had a guide to help us navigate the many hallways and rooms accessible to visitors. This time, the guide was ours alone. Our private tour was led by a very knowledgeable young man by the name of Ben. We found Ben in the crowds outside the Vatican by seeking out the "angel umbrella" he said he'd be holding. His umbrella featured Raphael Sanzio's iconic *cherubini* (the two-winged cherubs looking upward in his *Sistine Madonna* work of art). Like Finn, Ben was not native to Rome, but his knowledge and passion for this wonderful city and the Vatican, in particular, would rival that of anyone who had lived there since birth. Ben couldn't have been more than twenty, maybe twenty-two, years old, but he was passionate about his vocation as a Vatican representative.

Our day at the Vatican had an unexpected twist because we were joined by my father's friend Paolo and his fiancée, Ivana. They were traveling from Slovakia and decided to meet us. I was looking forward to seeing them, thinking it would be a nice break from all the family togetherness we'd been immersed in up until then.

Paolo and my father had become friends when my father was teaching English as a second language. A lifelong middle school science teacher, my dad took up teaching ESL when he retired. We had not seen Paolo in ten years, since he returned to his homeland of Slovakia. I always thought he was such a nice person. In a small-town girl kind of way, I felt rather worldly to be rendezvousing with friends on European ground.

Touring with Paolo and Ivana also offered a distinct perspective on the sights we were seeing. They were a young couple in love and on the verge of marriage. Their fresh interpretation and obvious enthusiasm was enjoyable to be around.

"Paolo, Ivana—you made it. It's so wonderful to see you," my father said while embracing them in a warm hug.

"Jim, you look good," Paolo said. "You've not changed a bit."

I'm sure my father appreciated his kindness. The reunion of old friends was nice to watch. When Paolo was in America getting to know my dad, I think he grew to see my dad in a fatherly way. My dad is forever teaching, so even when not leading a classroom, he doles out words of wisdom to anyone who will listen. As a young man finding his way in a foreign country, I'm sure Paolo truly appreciated the comfort of Dad's knowledge. Further pleasantries were exchanged, comments about how the kids had grown, and we all took a few minutes to catch up as best we could in the brief time we had before setting out for the day's tour.

Ten years. How did that happen? Paolo really hadn't changed. His tall, lean frame and strong facial features gave way to his kind eyes and sweet disposition, just as I'd remembered. Seeing him with Ivana, a natural beauty with similarly strong features and a most pleasant personality, was heartwarming and energizing. There was a different mood going into this day with our touring companions by our side. It was nice.

Once inside the Vatican, I immediately noted that it was like nothing I'd ever seen. The art, sculpture, design, architecture, and even landscaping were magnificent. And there was so much of it, so much that it was intimidating to ponder how we'd get through it all. Here's where not fully knowing what to expect when touring the Vatican can present a real problem. And I thought I was prepared! By the end of this possibly once-in-a-lifetime opportunity, I was ready to pass out both from heat exhaustion and, I'm embarrassed to say, boredom.

I'm not a history buff or anything even close (Bravo TV is kind of my bible—embarrassed again!), so the lengthy tour dumbfounded me. And when I say lengthy, I mean that Ben did not edit any part of his spiel for the sake of the hot and worn out crew before him. He was uber excited about sharing his knowledge, and it seemed that nothing, absolutely nothing, could hold him back. To make it even more challenging, Ben spoke rather softly and sweetly. Straining to hear his voice exhausted me more so than the heat and wearisome walking. As we toured the massive Vatican on foot, it wasn't long before I began missing those crazy golf carts. There were some moments when I could do nothing to mask my glazed-over expression. "Are you okay?" Tony asked at one point.

"Everything that Ben is saying is going in one ear and out the other. I am completely checked out, and I don't think I can check back in."

I hate that I do not have a longer attention span for information that is beyond my scope of interest yet valuable to have. I wish that when visiting one of the most significant places in the world, I could have appreciated it for every historic detail it presented to me.

My harsh reality is that I'm a limited person who simply cannot process such an overload of information all at once. Even though I loved looking at the art and architectural details throughout the Vatican (I'm a look first, learn later kind of gal), the abundance of it, accompanied by Ben's wealth of knowledge, was my undoing.

My appreciation for all things pictorial did come in handy, though, while Ben spoke in painstaking detail about almost every picture in what seemed to be over a thousand rooms. If you've been to the Vatican, you know that many of the rooms are filled from floor to ceiling with original paintings, each with valuable historical significance. Ben talked endlessly about way too many of them.

"Wow—that is unbelievable," Karla said while listening to Ben.

Snapping to attention, I asked, "What was? What did he say?"

"He said that if you were to look at each piece in the Vatican for only five seconds each, it would take over three months to view everything."

"Good God," was all I could conjure up in response, and then I realized I probably shouldn't say that here.

Soon after this, I went into self-preservation mode and tuned out the audio in favor of the amazing artwork all around me. I immersed myself into the spectacularly large pieces of art and came to my own conclusions as to what they were all about—all seventy thousand of them along the four-and-a-half-mile display.

I focused more on the artistry and less on the history of the artwork and marveled at how each canvas or sculpture was created with such amazing craftsmanship. I began to imagine what it would be like to have painted something so large, yet full of minute detail.

The Ceiling of the Gallery of Maps was one of the creations that left my mouth hanging open in awe.

It was elaborate, gold, and gorgeous, and it filled the arched ceiling of a lengthy hallway. The Hall of Statues was equally inspiring, with so many extraordinary sculptures gathered all in one place. I find collections of things to be far more interesting that anything in the singular, and this collection was unparalleled.

"Mommmm," a little voice moaned behind me. "How much longer are we going to be in here? I'm soooo tired."

My poor little Ally was reaching her breaking point. If only she knew that her mom was, too, and we were only about halfway through.

"Good God," I said again, this time under my breath.

Apparently, our close proximity to God in his primary residence on earth paid off, because my prayer for fresh air and distraction was soon answered. Our next stop was the outdoor Vatican Museum grounds.

The spacious courtyard featured a lush green lawn and paved pathways. In the center of the grounds was a jumbo spherical sculpture created for the Vatican Church in the 1960s by Italian sculptor Arnaldo Pomodoro. It is called the *Sphere within Sphere* or *Sfera con Sfera*. Pomodoro says that the inner ball represents the Earth and the outer ball represents Christianity. Pomodoro has gone on to replicate this sculpture for other prominent locations around the world, including the Headquarters of the United Nations in New York City, The Christian Theological Seminary in Indianapolis, and Tel Aviv University in Israel.

The unexpected artistry of this golden sphere was the perfect focal point to draw our attention and spark our energy. Studying the complex, gear-like innards of each sphere and imagining the smaller, inner sphere breaking out of the cracked shell of the outer one reminded me of a bird hatching from an egg.

While modern in style, it somehow suited the space and acted as a captivating centerpiece. Karla and Alex thought it resembled the Death Star from *Star Wars*.

The fresh air was just what I needed to perk up. I found myself suddenly so afraid of missing something that I became uncontrollably camera happy, which usually I am not.

"Mom, why are you taking so many pictures?" Julia asked. "Half the stuff isn't even important."

A child's questioning of a thoughtful parent has to be the most frustrating thing in the world. In her defense, though, I may have taken the picture taking a bit far. I just couldn't decide what would make a good photo, so I took pictures of everything. I can see now that it was annoying and pointless. I'm a horrible photographer.

Following the Vatican Museum, we were led to one of the most famous places in the world, the Sistine Chapel. I was surprised by how small it was, so intimate and ornate. Of course, we were jammed into the small space like sardines in a can. Guards repeatedly hollered, *"Silenzio!"* Only a moment of quiet was had before the crowd's resumed whispers escalated into a soft roar. All the while, my dad spoke at full volume, regardless. His father, my Papou, always did the same thing in church. The more we told him to be quiet, the louder he got.

We couldn't help but *ooh* and *aah* over seeing Michelangelo's floor-to-ceiling masterpiece firsthand. There were so many different images on every surface that it was hard to know where to look. The urge to snap a photo was inescapable. Capturing the chapel's famous ceiling for posterity seemed to be on everyone's mind as I spied several fellow sightseers, necks craned, poised to point and shoot if a moment allowed. The muted colors and lifelike images throughout the murals made all the artwork appear multidimensional. If only I could have, I would have reached out to touch the paintings just to prove that they weren't sculpture. Velvet rope stanchions prevented me from doing this while guards warned against any kind of photography.

Someone in our group overheard a tour guide mention that they were required to say that. He said that it would be okay to take a quick picture as long as you weren't overt about it. A rush of temptation came over me because I really wanted that picture, but at my core I'm a rule follower. I felt badly that we were in this sacred place with hundreds of people talking when we shouldn't be, and now I was scheming to take a photo? It just didn't seem right. "Guys," I whispered to Bob and Tony. "I really want this pic. Cover me."

"Do it, Betty," Bob encouraged. "It's fine. I've already taken a bunch."

I could have relied on Bob's secondhand pictures, but I really wanted this one for myself. I went ahead and took the photo. It was worth it, as I now look at that photo of the fingertips touching from *The Creation of Adam* and think to myself, I was there!

Our final destination at the Vatican was a self-guided walk through St. Peter's Basilica. Wow! What a place. Having the opportunity to say a quiet prayer inside these walls was deeply spiritual. What's more, this place, where I had never been and seen few pictures, held an air of familiarity the moment I walked through the door.

As we entered, Karla and I were immediately drawn to the right where, encased in glass, was Michelangelo's *Pietà*, a life-size, if not larger than life, sculpture of Mary holding a grown Jesus across her lap. It was beautiful, not only because of its subjects and mastery of craftsmanship, but because my parents had a miniature version of this very sculpture in their bedroom.

"Do you remember that little statue from Mom and Dad's room?" I asked Karla.

"Of course I do," she said. "It sat in that same spot on their bureau for years."

I wondered whatever happened to it and wished I could recover it as a keepsake.

In addition to this memorable work of art, I was also struck, if not taken aback, by the glass-encased, embalmed body of Pope John XXIII. Revered for his role as founder of Vatican II, this Pope was hugely popular. All I kept thinking was, is that his real body? It seemed strange to be standing

over someone who'd died in 1963. Pope John XXIII was can-
onized in 2014. St. Peter's Basilica was exceptional.

Finally, our Vatican tour reached its end. Our sweet but
very long-winded tour guide, Ben, took a few extra minutes
to close out the day while we overlooked St. Peter's Square
and the Vatican Obelisk (one of thirteen Egyptian stone pillars in Rome standing nearly one hundred feet tall). I was
beyond exhausted, overheated, and mentally tapped. I just
couldn't listen to another tidbit of history or unknown fact,
so I walked off without saying a word or even thanking the
poor guy. I feel guilty about it to this day. So, this is for Ben—
if he ever has the opportunity to read it:

*Thank you. Thank you for your patience, your passion, and
for the broad knowledge that you so admirably impart unto others. But mostly, I thank you for taking the time to lead three
generations on a tour that will forever be part of a special trip
that can never be replicated.*

7. Breathe

ROME TOOK MY BREATH AWAY. BOTH BECAUSE I was fully enthralled with my experience there and because it felt like I hadn't had the chance to catch my breath since I first began worrying about this trip over a year ago.

Before leaving Rome, we visited my sister's flat, where she and her family had chosen to stay instead of a hotel. We also took an evening stroll to the Trevi Fountain to make a customary wish.

I loved my sister's flat for its authenticity and European flavor. I imagined myself living there, and a warm feeling came over me. There was an ease and simplicity to it that appealed greatly to me. It was familiar, too, even though this was my first time setting foot there. Like on Ben's umbrella, wall art of the cherubims hung over the master bed. As my girls lay on the bed trying to replicate the scene of the well-known image, I felt oddly comfortable and normal, like I belonged there. I could feel Italy beginning to take hold of me.

Trevi Fountain

It was evening by the time we walked from the flat to the Trevi Fountain. It was crowded when we arrived, and I enjoyed the energy of being out and about. In front of the fountain is a pool of water where the masses of people around it can toss coins for good luck. The sunken position of the fountain from street level allows the steps down to the water's edge to act perfectly as stadium seating. More than a wishing well, it is a lively location to gather and hang out for a while. The rather loud sounds of rushing fountain water and the buzz of excited voices were not noisy like you might expect, but musical. There was an unmistakable electric energy in the air.

When we tired of people-watching, we stood together to do what we tourists come here to do: toss pennies over our shoulders. I made my wish, and on a count of three, our pennies were gone. I later learned that the coin toss is said to ensure you will return to Rome. I hope that comes true as well.

With the packed sightseeing schedule of Rome behind us and the pleasant opportunity to process our immense joy at being there in front of us, I felt the tension in my body slowly fade away.

In two short days, we made the most of Rome and embraced Italian culture as best we could. By that, I mean we wasted no time eating and drinking every Italian delicacy that we could get our hands on. To be clear, Tony and Bob did most of the drinking, but we were all in a celebratory state of mind.

Most of the grown-ups imbibed in typical fashion— reserving adult refreshments for dinners, happy hours, night caps—you get the idea. Bob and Tony, however, never missed a chance to sample a European beer, shot, or glass of vino. Lunch, brunch, dinner; it was all great timing for them. They are big guys, so they could handle it. I, on the other hand, would never make it out of my room if mimosas or Bloody Marys were on the menu before noon. Courtesy of Bob and Tony alone, we have so many photos of bottles of beer that I seriously thought about censoring the family photo album.

In one photo taken in Rome, snapped surreptitiously by Bob, Tony is pictured holding something in a shot glass alongside a waiter named Giorgio. This adorable Italian young man served us a wonderful meal after our day at the Vatican. It all felt very wholesome as we enjoyed our outdoor seating: Julia and Ally slurped spaghetti and Paolo and Ivana told us where they were headed after Rome. Meanwhile, inside, there was an impromptu celebration happening at the bar.

When I first opened the photo link that Bob sent me, and I saw this picture, I had to stop to think about where we were.

"Tony, why is it that no matter where we are or what time of day it is, you manage to make it a party?" I said, pointing to his photo with Giorgio.

"What do you mean? Oh, that. We just wanted to toast Giorgio for his great service."

When did Bob and Tony slip away from our quaint sidewalk table to sneak a shot of some random Italian spirit with the waiter? To think that we had just spent a holy day at the Vatican, complete with knees and shoulders covered!

Party boy mentality aside, the moment we set foot in Italy, we all took considerable pride in doing our very best to be gracious and polite. The last thing we wanted to be thought of was "ugly Americans."

Whenever appropriate and feasible, we spoke Italian, using basic terms like *grazie* and *prego*. At no point did it occur to me that this good-mannered habit would eventually present a slight annoyance. It seemed that one of our most ambitious family members—Tony—didn't recognize or care that only about a third of our trip would be so Italian-specific. Once we departed Italy, we boarded a cruise ship where passengers and crew had come from far and wide. The Greek mainland, three Greek Islands, and Turkey were also on our agenda. Yet none of this mattered to my over-achiever husband, who became so enamored with Italy that he decided to use his few Italian pleasantries on the cruise ship, in Greece, and in Turkey. He thanked absolutely everybody in Italian or randomly used the term *prego* at times when it wasn't appropriate.

"Tony, it's nice that you've embraced the Italian language with such zeal, but can you give it a rest?" I commented pointlessly. "You're not even using it correctly half the time."

"*Grazie,*" he said with a chuckle.

Following a trip to London a few years ago, Tony took a liking to the Brits' truncated version of "grocery store." They would just say "grocery." It took him a good six months to stop asking questions like, "When are you heading to the grocery?" or "I'm running to the grocery, do you need anything?" Thankfully, that ran its course without too much aggravation.

Similarly, Tony's Italian, while frequently out of place, did provide terrific opportunity for some lighthearted jabbing. He took it in stride, just as we did his new love of the Italian language.

By the time we boarded the ship, we had acclimated to the time change, and most of us (especially Tony) to any minor language barriers. We were physically and mentally prepared to get our vacation groove on. Rest, relaxation, and lounge chairs, here we come.

When we first set eyes on the Royal Caribbean Equinox Cruise Ship, the only words I could think to say were, "Holy crap! This ship is freaking huge." It was like a small city floating on water. The adults had all traveled by cruise ship before, but this was by far the largest ship any of us had been on.

How the heck do they do that? This was a question I would repeatedly ask myself regarding many of the sights and structures we saw that were so colossal or intricate that I could not imagine what it would have taken to construct them. Whether we were looking at the cruise ship, a Roman temple, or a meticulously carved statue, the creation of it baffled me.

The kids were in shock and mesmerized by the gargantuan boat.

"Is this our boat?" Julia asked. "It's massive. I don't get how something this size doesn't sink."

"Jujee!" I exclaimed. "Don't talk about sinking just as we are about to step on board."

I refused to get any further bogged down with worries because, like with flying, the more I thought about it, the more twisted my thoughts became.

Once officially on board and in our cabin, I was pleasantly surprised by the size of our quarters. Our suite was quite spacious. It had a master bedroom, a bunk bed compartment for the girls, a comfortable sitting area with a couch, two chairs and a television, a dining table, a small veranda, and of course, a bathroom. Wow—all of Tony's planning sure paid off.

The last time Tony and I cruised, we were on our honeymoon. Our cabin was so small that our bed barely fit. We had to squeeze and maneuver our way around the bed to get to the door and to gain access to the bathroom. Tony said it made him feel claustrophobic. I remember thinking he looked like a bear in a bird's nest.

Apparently, some things get better with age.

Finally getting settled into our cabin was a nice turning point as we prepared for the next phase of the trip. This would be our home for the next twelve days, and we were spending our first full day aboard at sea. All I could think about was doing a whole lot of nothing.

Our first night, however, after the whirlwind of unpacking, was spent celebrating the first of two birthdays on the high seas.

Our collective jubilation for our first "dressy" night dinner, in honor of my Mom's seventy-third birthday, reminded me of the flutter before prom. After a couple of hot and sweaty days of sightseeing, an elegant meal sounded nice.

We would also celebrate Bob's birthday six days later.

I found these "special occasion" dinners to be especially entertaining. Typically, sitting down to a fancy dinner with the kids is a balancing acting between best behavior, boring, and entirely not worth the aggravation and expense. Imagine a mouthful of delicious seafood risotto perched at my lips, ready to be savored, and just as I'm about to taste it, I hear, "Mom, are you almost done? How much longer do you think we'll be? I need to go to the bathroom. There's a show we want to watch at eight."

Offsetting mealtime malaise is just one of the advantages of traveling with kids of similar ages. Katherine, thirteen, and Alex, fifteen, were the perfect companions for Julia, twelve, and Ally, nine.

Katherine and Alex are Julia's and Ally's only cousins, and for this reason they are especially tight. Katherine is a go-getter, into everything from theater to crew to the latest girly trend. Although older than my girls, she is close enough in age for the three of them to get along famously. Each of the girls has long brown hair and big, doe-like eyes. When they are together, they are often mistaken for sisters.

Alex is tall, like his father, and similarly built like a football player. He is a jokester who is equally talented in the arts of Xbox and piano. He blows us away with his natural talent for tickling the ivories. My girls look up to both Katherine and Alex and love spending time with them.

It felt good to loosen the apron strings a bit on this vacation. With their cousins by their side, I did allow the kids to take off to explore the ship on their own. I had a few moments of silent panic occasionally, but I managed to let go of it once the peace and quiet of a kidless environment sank in. The more I relaxed, the more I realized that I worry too much. "Beth, you need to encourage the girls' independence," Tony always said. "You smother them."

"There is nothing wrong with encouraging power in numbers," I would say in return. No matter what the situation, I just felt better when they were part of a larger group.

Ostia Antica

This very point was proven in Ostia Antica, where we stopped just prior to arriving at the ship.

Ostia Antica is a vast archaeological site outside of Rome where hundreds of partial buildings remain standing for self-guided exploration. Though just thirty minutes from downtown Rome, it does not draw the kind of touristy crowd one might expect for such a remarkable sight. As you walk through the remains of this bygone community, it resembles a maze where rows of structures intertwine and go on for miles. Ostia was once ancient Rome's seaport where sixty thousand people resided. The bustling district was a thriving commercial port until the fall of Rome, when it was abandoned. Over time, the harbor filled with silt, leaving Ostia buried but preserved. Archaeologists began uncovering Ostia in the 1960s.

This was the most phenomenal representation of preservation we saw in Italy. I could not get over how large a colony it was for its time, dating as far back as fourth century BC. We walked for miles amid the archaeological remains of little brick dwellings, theaters, shopping centers, warehouses, and common areas. Marble bath houses, frescoes, and decorative mosaic floors rounded out the trek through time.

During our visit there, few other tourists were around. It was rather desolate, but intriguing nonetheless. We took our time admiring various nooks and crannies, and eventually detoured into the community theater area. To enter this space, we had turned right off the main drag and entered through the former front entryway. We were rather engrossed with what had once been the stage and the ample stone stadium stands that surrounded it. Bob wowed us with his demonstration of the acoustical efficiencies inside the amphitheater. While we stood at the top row of stadium seating, he spoke softly on the stage. We could hear him clear as day.

At this point, Ally somehow escaped my watchful eye and wandered ahead. When I realized that she was not with us, a lump formed in my throat, and my eyes began darting in every direction with the hopes of catching a glimpse of her.

"Where is Ally?" I snapped, hastily looking and repeating myself from one person to the next. While everyone else didn't appear to sense the urgency in my voice, Alex wasted no time and took off at a runner's pace to find her. He tore out of the theater without any hesitation. I quickly followed.

Thank God we didn't delay, because she turned up a good half a mile ahead of us.

"Ally," I shouted, "what are you doing? Why would you ever walk away on your own?"

"I was looking for the horses."

"What are you talking about?"

"The horses! Remember the guy at the front of this place said there are horses in here."

"No, I don't remember that! Oh my God." I was so freaked out—I didn't even remember "the guy."

It's no surprise that the horses never turned up. I was back to being breathless. Thank God, we were about to start the cruise portion of our trip.

With Alex and Katherine unknowingly working double duty as both security and entertainment for Julia and Ally, I was ready to kick up my heels and exhale.

8. Let It Go

THE FIRST MOMENTS ON THE SHIP WERE AS EXCITing as they were pacifying. It was nice to have a base to call home for the remainder of our trip. I gladly unpacked my bags and enjoyed the calm that washed over me.

"This is starting to feel good," I said to Tony.

"What do you mean?"

"Rome was great, but I feel like this is the real start of vacation, and I'm psyched to settle in."

"Well, you have ten days; make the most of it."

He didn't have to tell me twice. I was primed and ready. Did I really not want to go on this trip? Man, what was I thinking?

I admit I had reservations about the family trip. I questioned whether we'd get on each other's nerves. The last time I had spent this much uninterrupted time with my mother, father, and sister, I was fresh out of college living back at home. That lasted for six months until I hightailed it out of there to live out my early twenties with roommates. My twenties were the best years of my life. You don't have to be rich to have fun. I hoped I wouldn't want to get away from my family now. I had no place to go.

I didn't! In fact, I enjoyed the opportunity to spend quality time together and enjoy conversations that didn't need to be cut short because someone was running to a meeting, a bingo game, or dropping kids somewhere. Tony and I had occasion to walk and hold hands, and we even had a few double date nights with Karla and Bob. It was nice knowing the kids were together and content hanging out in our suite while my tired parents kept watch in the adjoining room. It was a refreshing break from the doldrums of home.

Another luxury of travel at sea was that it forced us to unplug. All our phones, computers, and games were inaccessible—a perfect inconvenience.

For a hefty price, we could've found a way to be connected, but none of us did.

Our technological limitation, or luxury, as I saw it, was most valuable for Tony. As a business owner, his career is all about his network, being connected, and staying in near constant contact with his partners, employees, clients, and prospects. His BlackBerry is with him always. As with so many other workaholics who find it hard to disconnect, it can be annoying for those around him—namely me. To see him detach and truly relax was a pleasure for me.

The one person on our trip who I thought would be the last to seek communication with home was my father. He would be the first to put everything else behind him and worry only about his immediate family. There was, however, one very important member of my father's world who didn't travel with us: his beloved ten-pound, fluffy white Shih-Poo named Buddy. My father adores this little dog, and leaving him for fourteen days was heart-wrenching for him. Dad couldn't possibly rest easy without knowing how his baby was doing. He approached Tony with the need to use the emergency-only track phone that Tony brought along for, as you might guess, emergencies only.

"Tony," Dad called, "you brought a phone, right?"

"Yes, but it's for emergencies only," Tony responded matter-of-factly.

"Well, can I use it?" asked Dad.

"Is it an emergency?" Tony shot back.

"It will be if you don't let me use it. Hand it over," Dad demanded.

Tony does not in any way share my father's love of animals, but he does love my father.

You might think the phone drama would end there, but no, there had to be some kind of *Seinfeld*-esque absurdity to follow. (My dad reminds me of George Costanza's father, Frank, played by actor Jerry Stiller.) The hand-off of the phone led to about fifteen minutes of confused outbursts as my seventy-five-year-old father attempted to execute the call.

"How does this thing work? Do I have to press a country code? Does it come with instructions? I think it's broken."

Dad never did get service on the track phone, but in a final attempt to fulfill his mission, he resorted to using the cruise ship's outrageously expensive telephone service. By the end of the cruise, he had charged numerous thirty-dollar phone calls that he told no one about until my mother came across the charges on their final bill. She was so annoyed, but I couldn't help giggling at how nuts my dad is.

Unplugging was great, but my personal moment of euphoria came when we returned to our cabin after our first dinner aboard. When I realized that our stateroom attendant, James, had been in to draw the drapes, tidy the entire cabin, refresh bathroom towels, wipe down the bathroom sink, turn down beds, and gift each of us with a lovely chocolate on our pillows, I felt truly spoiled, and I loved it.

"James is my new favorite person," I said as I plunged into bed. "I could really get used to this."

"Please don't," Tony pleaded.

Every time I saw James after that first night, I waved and smiled at him like he was my new best friend. You've got to love a guy who cleans up after you and leaves you chocolate.

I realized this is the kind of pampering every good vacation should have. I liked it, I needed it, and quite frankly, I deserved it. For years, we went back and forth to our lake house in New Hampshire, and that's what we called vacation. Having the house was a blessing, but being there involved the same cleaning, cooking, and schlepping we did at home. That's not a vacation, but this was, and for the first time in such a long time, I felt I was getting the break that every mother of young kids needs now and again.

The pluses of our trip far outweighed the minuses. But to be honest, I should share some of the cons that came along with the pros. At about four a.m. on the first morning, we pulled into the Sicilian port of Messina, and Tony and I awoke.

"What the hell is that noise?" I said.

"I have no idea," Tony responded.

Sounds of winding, whirring, clanking, and clashing ensued for what had to have been a half hour as the boat docked, and I finally identified the sound as the anchor. I realized we were on an insanely large ship, but in my weary, half-woken state I couldn't believe the anchoring process could possibly be this involved and piercing.

"God, just dock already," I wailed.

"Jesus, how long can this go on?" Tony groaned. "This is ridiculous."

It really was insane. Tony, typically the calm one and an early bird, was surprisingly frustrated.

I lay there trying to envision what was happening outside our cabin that would result in such a loud, long cacophony. I imagined crewmen scrambling about struggling with an anchor gone awry. In fact, I hoped they were having trouble anchoring at this port, meaning this would be a one-time occurrence. To make matters worse, the noises and motions repeated dozens of times before all returned to quiet. My notoriously limited patience was being tested.

I avoided mentioning the noisy incident to the girls, hoping that Tony and I had made more out of it than it really was.

"Good morning, ladies, how did you sleep?"

"Good."

"Yeah, good."

The brief pause and typically disinterested responses led me to believe we may have averted a crisis.

"Until all that noise started," Julia added. "It was sooooo loud and annoying."

"Oh my God, right," Ally said. "It was the worst ever, what was that?"

I couldn't help but wonder if this disturbance would be the undoing of our vacation. I imagined we'd wake to this incessant noise day after day and find ourselves tired and cranky. Wait, wasn't that how I usually felt at home and wasn't that exactly what I wanted to escape?

I stopped myself in my tracks. *No*, I told myself, *do not let this one thing derail a perfectly enjoyable experience.* In that instant, I did the exact opposite of what I would normally do and just let it go. The peaceful sensation that come over me was weird but oddly comfortable. My mind wasn't racing; I wasn't getting anxious, and I wasn't yapping incessantly about something I couldn't control.

Strangely, as if the travel gods were looking down upon us, we managed to tune it all out going forward. It still happened every single day, in the wee hours of each morning. I don't know if we were all purely exhausted or if we'd all reached such a zen state of vacation bliss that nothing could bring us down, but the noise didn't bother us past the first day.

"I can't believe I'm saying this, but I actually don't mind our noisy wake-up call," I said to Tony.

"Me either," he said. "I actually haven't really noticed it since the first day."

"I'm not surprised; your snoring may be drowning it out. Since I'm so used to that, I guess it's not so bad."

I found that the loud anchoring process got me up and going much earlier than I would have otherwise, and it gave me time in the morning to ease into the day. Rather than wake up, get ready, and rush out the door for an excursion, it was nice to have a few extra minutes each morning. We took the opportunity in the cabin to lounge around while we waited for the ship's signal that it was safe to cross the gangway. I ended up valuing that time. We purposefully didn't overbook ourselves from port to port, and we were left feeling unrushed and unstressed. We let go of the "jam-pack your life" mentality and took a "less is more" approach. That was the best thing we could've done.

9. Sicily

IF WE HAD ANY LINGERING CONCERNS ABOUT OUR morning's unconventional wake up call, they were completely forgotten when we arrived in Sicily. On this day, my sister and her family chose to hang back on the ship to recover from the first few days of active touring. The rest of us took off to Taormina, Italy, a small town on the east coast of Sicily, for a perfectly lovely day.

Within minutes of setting eyes on the cluster of hilly streets and quaint shops, I was completely taken with this little resort town.

Something about Italy, every part that we visited, spoke to me in a way that was undeniable. I felt a strange connection and sense of belonging with every step we took on Italian ground.

I thought about my Yia Yia, who'd have turned in her grave if she knew I were favoring my Italian sensibilities over my Greek ones. As far as she was concerned, all her grandchildren were one nationality and one nationality alone.

"You are Greek, don't forget it—Greek!" she would say. Always with a rolled "r" and heavy emphasis on the last "Greek."

Yet here in Italy, I felt so comfortable and at home. I wondered if motherhood had anything to do with the powerful draw I felt to this magnetic country. This may be a stretch, but the mother I am today is much more a reflection of my own, doting Italian mother than I ever imagined I would be.

Phrases like, "Girls, take one more bite of your dinner," and "Don't you talk back to me—who do you think you are?" and "Hate is a very strong word, you know," are all lines I have dished out to my daughters, just as my mother did to me. None of this is necessarily Italian, but the similarities bond me to my mother. Maybe, then, her Italian roots resonate more so within me.

While many women dismiss their maternal similarities, I smile whenever I hear myself sounding like my mother or mimicking her parenting style. I wouldn't have it any other way.

The people we encountered in Sicily, like those in Rome and every other stop we made in Italy, exuded a warm and welcoming vibe. While I found the beauty of the country to be exceptional, it was the inner beauty of the people that allowed Italy to win my heart. Their unwavering spirit of friendly hospitality couldn't have been more apparent than with the charming tour guides who took us through Taormina.

I don't know if it's typical to set up a private tour at each port, but we did, and it was well worth every extra dime we spent. The gentlemen, and I don't use that term lightly, took the utmost care in assuring that our time in Sicily was everything we could've hoped for. The experience would have been entirely different had we been part of a group tour.

All our guides in Italy and Greece were experts in their craft. They made our time in their countries far more compelling with every step we took. There were no forced pleasantries, either, as if to secure a better tip. Each guide was passionate about showcasing his beautiful city, town, or village in the most flattering of lights. Their passion showed in their expression, tone, thoughtfulness and, mostly, that light in their eyes that could only come from someone talking about something or someplace they truly love.

Ciro, our main guide in Sicily, and his associate, Rosario, were the first of our guides to make a lasting, personal impression. Personal because they felt less like tour guides and more like knowledgeable members of our own group. The way they walked with us rather than ahead of us and spoke to each of us individually really made a difference in how we experienced Taormina. They were extremely engaging, which left me feeling a deeper connection with them.

Rosario did not speak English and no one in my party spoke Italian, yet it made no difference whatsoever. What could've been an awkward language barrier turned out to be nothing of the kind.

Rosario managed to help us appreciate all that we were seeing through his kind gestures. If he wanted us to look through a shop window, he would take one of us by the hand and lead us directly to the sight. If he thought a scene was photo-worthy, he would raise his hand to stop the group and take one of our cameras to snap the shot himself. He was adorable, and I made sure to turn the tables on him several times to get him in our family photo album as well.

Ciro was remarkably well-informed. He provided us with just the right amount of detailed commentary coupled with sightseeing visuals to create a perfect balance. We saw the Ancient Teatro Greco (Greek Theater) of Taormina where, from the highest point, you can look out onto Mount Etna and the colorful Sicilian landscape that beautifully frames the volcano.

We spent time with Ciro high in the stands of the great amphitheater as he told us about the theater's architecture, history, and modern-day use as an opera and musical performance venue. To get to the theater, we had to walk up a side street with a moderate pitch. The leisurely pace allowed us the chance to absorb the collection of buildings that snugly lined the streets.

Most eye-catching, for me, were the iron balcony railings. These decorative barriers drew my gaze up as I admired their many shapes and sizes. Some were bowed with curved ends, while others were linear with geometric patterns between each post. All featured bountiful planters filled with flowers and foliage that trailed down and over the sides of the railings. The depth of character in everything I saw gave me the feeling that this would be a happy place to live.

While in Taormina, we also peeked at the Palazzo Corvaja, a medieval Sicilian palace. The stonework, detailed arched windows, and signature crenellation (the gapped rampart around the rooftop) were enchanting, much like the fairy-tale castles I'd seen so many times in movies and storybooks. Seeing these historical places shaped the day into one that was valuable, educationally as well as personally.

The personal enjoyment came from Ciro's and Rosario's acceptance that the ladies of our group were desperate to sneak a little shopping into this day. Taormina is known for its quaint boutiques, and we wanted to be entirely sure we had ample time to take advantage of that. When the time to shop arrived, all the men were happy to make themselves scarce. They took off together to a nearby watering hole to relax and sip a few beers while the girls got our fill of the eclectic array of boutiques.

Taormina gave us our first taste of European shopping. Hundreds of little shops lined the main street called Corso Umberto. At first approach, the view of Corso Umberto looked like a textured oil painting: colorful, layered, and undeniably charismatic.

As we peered into store after store, we coveted everything from pink coral jewelry and handmade clothing to beautiful pottery and shoes, so many shoes. I was happy.

The road was also lined with eateries, trees, little gardens, window boxes, and potted plants that made our visit much more than a spending spree.

It seemed that no matter where on the street we were, there was something worth stopping to admire. Lush topiary gardens speckled with tiny red flowers between the shops on the sloping hillside stopped us in our tracks. The piazza (city square), where you could rinse your hands in a beautiful fountain that was there for the express purpose of refreshing weary walkers, was the perfect place to rest and take in the scenic views of the Ionian Sea. Spectacular views of the Mediterranean coast and Mount Etna surrounded us at varied points along our route.

My favorite keepsake from Taormina is a beautiful piece of pottery featuring Italy's signature fruits: lemons and oranges. We saw them growing on many Italian street corners. It was all I could do to keep myself from plucking one fresh off a branch. I had been on the lookout for a new piece of pottery to add to a collection I have at home, and when I stumbled upon this particular shop, I knew I should purchase a piece there.

The shop, called Di Blasi Ceramics, located about midway down Corso Umberto, was filled with stacks and stacks of handmade painted pottery. Every inch of every wall was covered in hanging plates, and the shelves were fully stocked. I liked that in this shop pottery wasn't just one of many other souvenirs being sold. Here, it was the main attraction.

The piece of pottery I bought that day is now hanging in my dining room along with sixteen other pieces I've picked up during my travels. Every time I look at the lemons and oranges on that plate, wonderful memories of our time in Taormina and Sicily come back to me.

After a solid stint of shopping, the girls, my mom, and I shared some Italian delicacies. We delighted in bites of arancini (rice balls—yum!), calzone, and, of course, something sweet—gelato again. We then reunited with the men, our purchases proudly in hand.

"*Ciao*, ladies," said Ciro. "I see you made the most of your time."

"Always," I said triumphantly while hoisting my swag for all to admire. "And how about you gentlemen?"

"We had a wonderful time," Tony chimed in. "Ciro and Rosario brought us to this great little pub. We had a few beers and learned more about Sicily."

"It was really wonderful, Beth," my father added. "Now let's go."

That seemed about right. When Dad is done, he's done, and it appeared that time had arrived, but not without one final stop.

Before returning to the ship, Ciro and Rosario drove us to a little Sicilian village perched at the top of a mountain. It was so remote that it was hard to believe people lived there. The winding roads that led to the top left all of us feeling a bit dizzy, never mind the ride down, which gave us the sensation that we were on the downslide of a rushing roller-coaster. But it was worth it.

This village was so removed from everything that it took on a very private vibe, almost as if we shouldn't have been there. When we arrived, the town seemed like it was asleep. We walked through its miniature church and shops and poked our noses into a tiny restaurant or two. We didn't go into them, but just perused each establishment because it seemed these places weren't for tourists; they were for the people blessed enough to actually live there.

In this little village that seemed to touch the clouds, fig trees grew out from the sides of stone walls. Stucco homes were lined with delicate red flowering plants. The church, while empty, was alive with fresh flowers and lit candles. Intricately designed walkways in diamond, zigzag, and checkered patterns offset the simple surroundings, making us aware that extraordinary pride was taken in this little place. It was a perfect ending to our day. It left me wanting more, but time would not allow it.

"Ciro, thank you so much for bringing us here," I said. "I imagine most people visiting Sicily wouldn't know to come here."

"Oh, no," Ciro said. "This is a special place that I bring only special clients. I want you to see the real Sicily."

When we returned home to Massachusetts, we heard from Ciro, who inquired about our travel impressions of Sicily. He asked if I would provide him with feedback from our time together. I was more than happy to accommodate his request. Sharing our wonderful experience with other travelers on his website, sicilyroutes.com, was my way of giving back and expressing my appreciation. This is what I wrote:

June 2012

Where to begin? Seeing Sicily alongside the knowledgeable and charming Ciro was an experience never to be forgotten. My entire family was thrilled with every aspect of this wonderful day in Italy. Ciro and his colleague, Rosario, kept a perfect pace for the three generations to see and enjoy all the breathtaking sights of Sicily. The extraordinary shopping in Taormina, the amazing views of a tiny, mountaintop village, and all the other stops along the way were made even more memorable with Ciro and Rosario leading the way. They filled our day with a balance of history, entertainment, and leisurely sightseeing. We could not have been happier to have them as our guides. It was everything we had hoped it would be and would highly recommend contacting Ciro to plan a future tour. We look forward to returning and connecting with Ciro again.

With fond memories,
Beth and Tony Daigle & Family

10. Don't Fill Up on Bread

WE WERE NOW ON DAY SIX OF OUR GETAWAY AND had seen two out of three destinations in Italy. Right about now, on any other week-long vacation, I'd be thinking and stressing about getting home. But with Greece, Turkey, and one more stop in Italy still to come, worrying was the last thing on my mind.

Despite looking forward to what was ahead, I felt a wave of fatigue come over me. I hoped this was just a fleeting response to my sudden change in lifestyle. I noticed my family members exhibiting similar signs—a collectively slower pace, less animated expressions, and far less chattiness. From the start, we were playing catch up from the six-hour time difference, but it was more the heat and ambitious touring that took the greatest physical toll. Yes, the physical exertion was daunting but, more than that, I found the feeling of being endlessly "on" to be even more depleting. The near constant talking, the intent listening to our guides, and the ultimate overstimulation as we attempted to absorb every little detail of our new surroundings was downright draining. As yet, there had been little downtime, and it may be that the mental fatigue slowed us down more than the physical. I was ready for a break.

I expected and hoped that our first full day at sea after Sicily would give me what I was searching for. I wanted to achieve that same sense of catatonic calm I experience at home when I settle in after a long day and can finally sink into my couch to watch one of my favorite shows. In the simplest of terms, I needed to zone out for a while.

Thinking back to my honeymoon cruise, I have to laugh at what fools Tony and I were to not appreciate the downtime of cruise life. What the heck were we always in such a rush to get to?

Now, after fifteen years of marriage and in the throes of parenting tween girls, Tony and I wanted nothing more than to sit our tired butts down and not move. I can't say whether every cruise demands such downtime, but on a trip like this, where we'd been touring for up to six hours a day in very hot weather, a lull in activity was very much needed and appreciated. Our days at sea weren't quite what I had imagined them to be—me in a large-brimmed sunhat, a chaise lounge, a fruity beverage complete with cocktail umbrella in hand and quiet moments gazing out to the peaceful blue ocean— but they certainly weren't bad. It would probably be tough for reality to meet my glamorized expectations. We took full advantage nonetheless; we ate, participated in ship activities, shopped, gambled (Bob and Tony), or just hung out. Our sea days did what we needed them to do between ports, and we always came away ready for the next round of sightseeing. In addition to getting off our feet, we used the time on board to catch up as a family and bond in a way that our busy lives at home didn't allow us to do. There is something to be said about spending time together with no real purpose other than being in each other's company and enjoying whatever's happening at any given moment.

Pool Time

Dips in the pool, lounging poolside, or simply finding a quiet spot on the boat to sit back and read a good book were the idealized images I had swimming around in my head when I imagined what my days at sea would look like. I'd seen my share of cruise commercials, and I had every intention of living the fantasy. However, my plan was quickly derailed when I realized that rest and relaxation on a cruise ship is not as easily achieved as one might think.

"Looks like we are a little late getting to the pool," I said to Karla and Katherine as they approached Julia, Ally, and me. "There is literally not one open seat."

"There's got to be something," Karla said. "Come on; let's walk around and look again."

Loop one, loop two, loop three. Nothing, nothing, and nothing.

"What time do these people get up to reserve a spot out here?" I asked. "I guess we can just grab towels and sit on the pool's edge."

"Okay," said Karla. "As long as you don't mind sandwiching yourself in between that guy with the speedo and that girl with her tatas hanging out."

Yikes! The scene at the pool was really something else, and I quickly learned that cruise aficionados will get up at the crack of dawn to secure their preferred poolside seating. We had missed that boat big time.

As we sat together dangling our feet in the water between speedo guy and tata girl, I contemplated going for a swim. I kept thinking about it and just couldn't bring myself to do it. Why? Well, to begin, the pools on this enormous boat were surprisingly small, and boy, were they crowded. There was a total of three. Two were outside—one right next to the other. The separation was so small, it just seemed like one pool. The third pool was inside the solarium, a glass enclosed, temperature controlled quiet area where a lot of the older cruisers liked to congregate. We found it to be too hot and dim, and our intent was to be outside enjoying the sun, so the solarium pool, while less crowded than the other two, was no more inviting.

I understand that you can't take up the ship's valuable real estate with oversize pools, but considering the substantial number of people expected to use pools on sea days, our two pool options on the Equinox were unquestionably limited.

The real issue here was not the size of the pools, but rather the masses of cruise goers who happily swam along in each other's company. There were so many people in the pool at one time, all I could think about was a sink full of dishes. I don't consider myself a germaphobe, but I must admit that when I saw the large number of kids, adults, and older folks all stewing together in what I imagined to be a cesspool of germs, I just couldn't bear the thought of diving in.

"You going in, Mom?" Julia asked.

"Um, not right now. You know me, it takes a while to warm up. I'll just dangle my feet for now."

"Warm up? It's like a hundred degrees out here," she said.

"Come on, Beth, go in," Karla said with a shady grin.

I gave her a look as dirty as I thought the pool water was, and she thankfully didn't push any further. She knew exactly what I was thinking because, unlike me, she's an actual germaphobe.

If the overfilled, cool waters of the pool weren't enough to keep me at bay, I didn't even want to think about the hot tub. Here we had an even smaller space, with hot tubbers practically lined up to squeeze in, shoulder to shoulder, thigh to thigh. Add heat to the water, and my hesitation increased with every glance of rising steam. All of this probably sounds ridiculous, but I claim a bad hot tub experience as my excuse. It was Julia's experience, but I promise, when your five-year-old child begs and pleads to go in a hot tub, and you give in against your better judgment, only to have that same child exit the hot tub with a prickly red rash that doesn't go away for a week, you too would be hot-tub averse.

If that memory wasn't enough, cruise ship staff would not let you forget that germs were indeed lurking around every corner. No matter where you turned, they were there, armed with hand sanitizer, happily dispensing it by the globfuls. "Washy, washy," they'd say as they slipped a squirt in your palm, whether you wanted it or not. By the end of the cruise, I made a game out of dodging them and living on the edge with my dirty hands.

With these thoughts and reminders that germs were wafting and swimming all around us, I decided my safest bet was to sit poolside, not touch anything, and chill out for a bit.

Well, maybe "chill" isn't quite the word to describe what goes on at the pool deck—not on this cruise anyway. What I learned rather quickly, as I attempted to enjoy a peaceful poolside snooze, was that relaxing on a cruise ship means very different things to different people. I'm not sure if it was this specific cruise line or the time of year we traveled, but quiet time was not the primary goal.

My dream was to be the lady in the large straw hat holding a frozen drink with a cocktail umbrella. Meanwhile sounds of chirping seagulls and crashing waves would serenade me as I peered peacefully into the big, blue ocean.

It wasn't like that. Instead, I was "entertained" by mind-numbingly loud music that was deafening and shockingly constant. To add to the fun, the DJ frequently spoke over the music with annoying little quips and party anthems.

"Hey y'all, you ready to get the party started? Don't forget to get your drink on at the bar with today's special cocktail. Do I see some dancers on the deck?"

Haven't these people ever enjoyed the splendor that is silence? At one point I became so audibly overstimulated that I shoved my headphones in my ears just to settle the noise level down. The reality on the cruise was that on sea days, when everyone was on board, there was a lot of activity and hype that was nearly impossible to escape. In my travel journal, I noted the noise level on the pool deck to be obnoxious, which was really a shame. There should be more quiet poolside spots on cruise ships where old farts like me can just relax and enjoy the sun, sea air, and sweet silence.

Fine Dining

When sea days turned to sea evenings, our mood quickly went from lackadaisical to lively. For the most part, we dined together as a family in the ship's formal dining room. It felt like a special occasion every night. One evening, however, Karla, Bob, Tony and I planned a double date dinner at the ship's finest restaurant, Murano. This was a pleasant change from the group dinners.

My sister and I have always had a good relationship. Like most sisters, we fight. I once drew a knife and she a marble rolling pin in an epic battle that left me locked inside the bathroom until one of my parents got home. The knife and rolling pin were never used, but we had an awesome flair for the dramatic in the hours we were home alone after school. In many ways we are nothing alike, but she is the one person who can make me laugh like nobody else. You might think that at an elegant dinner we would control our giggly ways, but why should this occasion be different than any other?

While we've always been similar in our ability to find humor in most things, mostly ourselves, we are quite different at our cores. Growing up, I was more sporty and preppy while Karla was more into heavy metal and makeup. I was an open book and she was quite closed. I was always getting into trouble and she was a master at keeping her teenage mischief under wraps. Despite our differences, we share the same core values instilled in us by our parents and the nuns who slapped our wrists over the course of nine years in Catholic school. More than anything, we are connected by our love of laughter.

I was looking forward to a nice night together with Karla and Bob and Tony, who'd be Bob's perfect dinner companion. Bob is one of the nicest guys, which makes me happy when he and Tony spend time together. You are only as good as the company you keep, right?

Bob affectionately refers to me as "Betty," and I prefer to call him Bobby. He is so persuasive when he speaks, sometimes we just go along with him. This was the case with Bob's ongoing mispronunciation, or as he might say, preferred pronunciation, of the word "Euro."

From the moment we were all together in Rome, whenever we referenced the European form of currency, Bobby would chime in with an oddly confident "*oyro,*" complete with a rolling "r" and a long "o." This was Bob's version of Euro, and he solidly stood by it. I heard it multiple times prior to our Murano dinner, but it wasn't until that night, and a few hearty glasses of wine, that I conjured up enough curiosity to lean in to my sister and ask, "Seriously, what the hell is he saying?"

This set off a firestorm of hysterical laughter and banter that would lead us to a guy versus girl wager as to how Euro should properly be pronounced. While other couples in the restaurant were quietly, some romantically enjoying their meal, we somehow found ourselves in a fit of laughter, placing bets on proper or improper pronunciations. All along, Karla and I knew we were right and we even got affirmation from a waiter, but in typical male fashion, Bob and Tony banded together, to this day insisting that Bob's "*oyro*" is the true way to say it.

The fun didn't end there, but maybe it should've. If I learned nothing else on this cruise, it was that you mustn't fall victim to a fool's rush. The cuisine at this fine dining restaurant was exceptional. Everything was delicious and refined, from the mouthwatering artisanal breads to the flaming cherry dessert. I didn't want to miss a thing, including the bread. Typically, I avoid bread before a meal. Not because I'm counting carbs, but because from the time I was little, a voice in my head would always caution me against this unwise overindulgence. It was my dad's voice, and it wasn't always in my head.

"Girls, don't fill up on bread, you are going to ruin your appetite!" he would exclaim whenever Karla or I would go for a piece.

God, it drove me nuts as a kid—I remember it like it was yesterday. Oh, that's because it was yesterday. Even now, my dad reminds me not to fill up on bread.

"Dad, I'm over forty, for the love of God. It's okay if I eat a second piece of bread."

I almost never do, though. Karla, on the other hand, forges her own path. She had a second piece of bread that night at Murano, if not a third and a fourth. She insisted on getting a taste of each type of bread in the basket. I suspect she had more than just a taste.

"You know what Dad would say if he were here," I said to Karla.

"I know, I know." She waved me off.

We went on to order, and when our meals arrived, we all dove in. Karla's dish was particularly impressive—filowrapped chateaubriand with cabernet sauce and béarnaise. I was slightly jealous.

When I stopped to take a breath, I caught a glimpse of my sister fidgeting in her chair. I noticed her pushing her food around her plate with her fork. I knew it! I looked at her and smiled.

"Why aren't you eating?" I asked, already knowing the answer.

"Oh, it's nothing," she said. "Just taking a breather."

"Why is your plate still full of food?"

"Oh my God," she whispered in a giggly but horrified way, "I think I filled up on bread!"

11. Athens

"I'M SO EXCITED TO FINALLY SEE GREECE," I SAID TO my father. "I can't believe it took me forty-two years to get here. You should've taken me sooner."

"Just be glad you're here now, okay?"

Dad's always such a lovable grouch.

Seeing this place that I'd heard and learned so much about was something I'd waited half a lifetime for. In a small way, I felt my arrival in Greece would be a homecoming to the stories of my grandparents and great-grandparents.

"Dad, do we still have family here?" I asked.

"I don't know."

"What do you mean, you don't know? Do we or don't we?"

"We do, but they are very distant."

"It might've been cool to reach out to them."

"Oh, God, no, I wouldn't want to do that," he said. "It would be too much work, and I'd be stuck having to do all the talking for us. Don't worry about any relatives. I'll show you everything you need to see."

Relatives or no relatives, Greece turned out to be a meaningful part of our journey. It wasn't effortless, and it challenged my expectations like no other destination before or after, but I felt complete for having seen it.

I suppose the fantasy of Greece that I'd created in my mind would have been hard for any reality to live up to. I'm not saying it wasn't great, but not quite as life changing as I thought it would be. For me, the pivotal moment in Greece came early in our travels there. The place I most wanted to see was the Parthenon. The image of this massive temple had always been distinctly emblazoned in my brain. The notion of seeing it and walking through the sacred grounds of the Acropolis became something of a quest. From the time I was a little girl, my family, including aunts, uncles, and cousins, would spend time together flipping through my Yia Yia and Papou's photo albums. They traveled a lot, and while their photos from Spain, Hawaii, and many other places were fun to look at, nothing stuck with me more than the photos of their trips to Greece. Something about their proud expressions as they stood together, most often with my grandmother's sister Stella, left me with a powerful desire to go where they'd gone and see what they saw. I always knew that someday I would see the Parthenon myself.

My grandparent's photos of this prominent example of historical architecture have always remained at the forefront of my memory. The same is true for a piece of jewelry that my mother and aunts each wear to this day. They are gold pendants, probably about two inches in diameter, each featuring a dazzling rendition of the Parthenon. My Yia Yia gifted one to each of her three daughters-in-law. Each woman, none of whom is Greek, has always worn hers with pride.

Upon arriving in the vicinity of the Acropolis, a hot trek up the hill to see the hallowed grounds and the Parthenon itself was required. This day, more than any other, was super steamy. So much so, I could see the haze in the air. The temperature had to have been in the mid-nineties, if not higher.

I'm strong in many ways, but heat is my kryptonite. I may be the only New Englander whose least favorite season is summer. I just can't handle the unrelenting sun. While others thrive in the warmth of the summer months, I slowly fade away, trudging through the heat and humidity, desperately awaiting the arrival of fall.

Trying to shake off my funk, I forged ahead. Beautiful Kalamata olive trees grew in groves all around us. Stray dogs slept in any shady area they could find. The ten-minute walk seemed much longer in the heat, but we were all thrilled to at last set our eyes on the Parthenon at the top of the hill.

"What the hell?" I scowled as I first laid eyes on the structure. "You've got to be kidding me."

The entire face of the Parthenon was covered in scaffolding.

I had expected this to be a real aha moment. Instead, the words I blurted out were, "This is such an eyesore—I am so disappointed."

Apparently, the Parthenon had been under renovation for eight years. Unfortunately, none of our travel literature had alerted us to this fact. Not that we wouldn't have come, but at least we could have altered our expectations accordingly.

"I can't believe this," I said to everyone in my party. "This is such a letdown!"

"I know, what a shame," Karla said with a dismayed, if not disgusted, tone.

"Would you two relax?" my Dad said dismissively. "It's fine. You can see through the scaffolding, and you know what it looks like anyway."

I suppose that was one way to look on the bright side, but this wasn't my dad's first time seeing it, so I don't think he fully understood quite how markedly that moment had fallen short of my expectations.

Adding to our lackluster first sighting of the Parthenon was the undeniable feeling that we'd been packed into the walking paths like sardines in a tin can. We were part of a ten-body thick, three-hundred-yard lengthy line full of tourists anxious to see this ancient citadel. Tony said, "I hate feeling like I'm part of a herd," and boy, did it ever feel that way.

I was later told that if you can arrange to visit the Acropolis in the early morning before the tourists disembark their cruise ships, that's the most peaceful and fulfilling way to experience this sight. That was obviously not an option coming off our cruise ship, but a nice idea if we were ever to travel back.

Once I got past the sinking feeling of a moment lost, never seeing the Parthenon of my mind's eye, I was able to move on and see the rest of the Acropolis in all its marvelous ruin.

As with many things we had already seen on this trip, the scale and craftsmanship of the dilapidated architecture on these ancient grounds was astonishing. The detailed fluting of columns, the decorative carving and the larger than life sculpting of historical Greek figures was incredible. I marveled at all of it set atop this mini-mountain overlooking a major city. Scaffolding aside, it was awe-inspiring.

Not so thrilling was the moment we realized we had lost my father amid the thousands of people across approximately eight acres of land. We had all been so engrossed in exploration, we never noticed he was gone. Isn't that what you usually say about little kids? And no, my father does not have even the slightest touch of Alzheimer's or dementia.

"Have you seen Dad?" Karla asked, sounding slightly exasperated.

"He was just with us a few minutes ago. When did you see him last?" I asked.

"It was more than a few minutes ago, I can tell you that," my mother huffed. My mother does not at all appreciate my father's tendencies to take off on his own. But honestly, after all the years he's done it, shouldn't we be used to it by now? Group activity isn't always Dad's "thing," so when he's had enough, he's quite comfortable veering off on his own.

"Just give it a couple of minutes," I said. "He'll turn up."

I always give my dad the benefit of the doubt. I get him; I am him. I knew he'd be fine.

This minor distraction became more nerve-racking as the minutes passed and my dad's silvery white head didn't promptly reappear. His signature white hair has acted as a beacon in the night for us on more than a few occasions. After a few loops around the tourist path and a good deal of anxious standing around, we decided it would be best to venture downward to meet our tour guide. We were obviously not going to leave my dad behind, but we were ready to go. The anxious waiting game just got annoying.

He did turn up, of course. In fact, he reached the van ahead of us. As we approached, he looked unaware that his departure was anything but ordinary.

"Dad, where were you?" Karla scolded.

"What do you mean? I was here."

"We were looking all over for you. You've been gone for over twenty minutes."

"Oh, for Heaven's sake Karla, I had to use the bathroom," he scoffed. "I'm a grown man; I know what I'm doing. Why are you always pestering me?"

"Could you have at least told someone?"

"How could I? I didn't know where any of you were."

These conversations are so ridiculous, I don't know why any of us still engage in them.

Not to be outdone by a brief missing person incident, Athens continued to make its mark on our travel chronicles. It was a provocative city that, at the time of our visit in 2012, was dealing with a significant amount of political strife. The general vibe and warmth of the Athenians was not the same as what we'd experienced in Italy, but that didn't detract from our time there. Another gifted tour guide named George helped us make the most of our day.

George drove us all over the city. One thing many of us commented on was the large amount of graffiti that covered many buildings that otherwise seemed well maintained.

"It's awful that so many buildings are defaced liked that," Tony said. "It's everywhere and looks terrible."

Some might call it ugly or messy, others might say it's art, but when I looked at it, I saw voices longing to be heard. The energy throughout Athens was strained. In fact, our response to everything we saw was more emotionally charged because of the underlying tension.

We watched the changing of the guards in front of the Greek Parliament building at Syntagma Square, where a large protest had taken place just days before. This was a theatrical ritual that featured young soldiers outfitted in traditional uniforms, *fustanella,* consisting of white pleated kilts, the Evzone's hat, wool tights, and the *tsarouchia*—traditional shoes with tufted toes. With the uncomfortably hot weather, it was hard to believe that these young men could go through such an elaborately choreographed routine without so much as a droplet of visible sweat. I loved being so close to their performance that I could see their composed manner and perfect posture. If they were sweating under their gear, their cool expressions never let on. They were like toy soldiers.

We also went underground to see the newly constructed subway system.

This seemed an odd stop, but it's where George took us, so down we went without fully understanding what we were about to see. George was a great guide, but he didn't over talk any of the things we were doing or places we were seeing. He got us where we were going and let us make our own judgments.

The transportation system itself was typical.

It turns out that the interest was not in the subway itself, but in what was uncovered and preserved during its construction. When the tunnels were dug, workers discovered many ancient artifacts. But rather than push past their findings or pull them out to be placed in a library or government building, the items were preserved where they were found and remain on display inside the subway terminal.

"Eeew," I heard from Katherine. "That's so gross."

I saw all the kids peering into what looked like a wall.

"What is it? Let me see," said Ally and Julia in unison.

"It's a skeleton," said Alex. "So cool."

Encased in glass was a skeleton that had been unearthed and left undisturbed in its final resting place. "How bizarre," I said to Tony.

"Why do you say that that?"

"The idea that someone's bones are considered art, and for some reason I can't look away. It's kind of strange. It's a little bit creepy and interesting at the same time."

Another memorable sight while driving through Athens was the sculpture *Dromeas* ("The Runner"), located outside the Athens Hilton on Vassilissis Sofias Avenue. This thirty-foot piece of art was completed in 1994 by Costas Varotsos and is a stunning depiction of a man in motion, created with layers of dark green glass. The convincing effect was fascinating, despite only driving by it.

It was nice to see a modern-day piece of art rival some of the ancient works we'd seen with its magnificence and craftsmanship. It made me think, yeah, we've still got it—even in the new millennium.

Our next stop was Panathenaic Stadium, where events for the 2004 summer Olympics were held. This is also the place where the Olympic flame is set before moving to the host city for all Olympic Games. The clean lines and simplicity of this venue were surprisingly modern in character. It had been reconstructed multiple times since its creation in the fourth century, and in the late nineteenth century it was updated to its current form. Aesthetically, it reminded me more of something I'd see in the United States. Then I thought about its enormity and that it's the only stadium in the world made completely out of marble, and I was quickly brought back to big, beautiful Greece.

Olympic Stadium did not hold our attention for long. Maybe if it hadn't have been so hot, I could have run the track and felt like I was reliving some athletic feat, but I was extremely drained and had to reserve my resources for the remainder of the day.

Things perked up when we arrived at the lesser-known Temple of Zeus. Getting away from the crowds and out of the van gave me just the boost I needed. I was happy to be one of few walking around this area. A break from the herd was a welcome and sanity-saving retreat. Here in the middle of the busy city of Athens was this wide-open land, on which stood the remains of the temple dedicated to the Greek God.

"I wonder where everyone else from our cruise ship is right now," Tony said.

"I know, right? It's strange that we are the only ones here," I said.

"This is why I reserved private tours. It gives us the chance to get away from everyone else."

"Thank God! I couldn't deal with crowds like at the Acropolis. This is good."

Zeus's temple lies on low land that has a clear view up the hillside to the Acropolis. The Parthenon was in plain sight from our vantage point and, for a moment from where I stood, I felt like I was seeing the Parthenon as I had imagined it in my mind for so many years.

The loftiness of the hill's peak seemed a likely place for a building as significant as the Parthenon. But the accessibility of Zeus's Temple, on level ground and nearer modern-day activity, had a very real and down-to-earth appeal. To envision this temple as part of the mainstream walk of historic Grecian life was intriguing to me.

"Mom, take a picture of us!" the girls shouted as my mind snapped back into reality.

"Look at how tiny we look next to the pillars," Ally said.

"We're like Lilliputians," added Julia.

The columns are nearly sixty feet high, and without the crowds like those at the Parthenon, we could take the time to absorb the massiveness of it all.

One of the columns that had collapsed in 1852, when the temple was pillaged in a barbarian invasion, was as mind-blowing as those that remained upright. The downed column lies on the ground, broken into uniform segments of limestone covered in stucco. It looked like carefully sliced pieces of salami laid out to serve at a cocktail party. I must've been getting hungry to think that.

Seeing the column broken into pieces made it clear that they had been constructed by stacking slices on top of each other, one by one. How the ancient Greeks got those colossal pieces to the top of each column remains a mystery to me. I'm sure the technique is detailed somewhere, but in a way, keeping the mystery alive is more exciting.

Walking through the remaining grounds of the Temple, we came across little gardens, or shrines, where small bits of preserved carvings, plaques, statues, and stones had been collected. I found myself lingering around these historical remnants, wondering how they got there and who made them. There was something peaceful in quietly contemplating the artistry and creation of each piece. Unlike my Vatican experience, I was not overwhelmed here.

At this point, George had taken a break and allowed us the opportunity to venture off on our own. Without him there to guide us and share information, we just enjoyed this place for what it was and what we could see. Like many of the "off path" places I've come to adore, I found Zeus's Temple to be more compelling than some of the better-known attractions.

With my mind already drifting to food, the timing was perfect for lunch. Mealtime was another instance when having a private tour guide proved to be a very good thing.

George avoided the typical touristy dining spots and brought us to a little hole-in-the-wall restaurant that far exceeded our expectations.

This hidden gem was in more of a business district, on a side street, tucked in among other types of business. The sign on the door read 5Φ which, as I understand, translates to 5F, or more likely, 5 Friends. The restaurant's name was followed by a long string of Greek letters which translated to "Traditional Restaurant."

5Φ was run by a man named Costas, who was the ideal maître d'. Costas was young, maybe late twenties, early thirties, with the thick head of black hair I've come to expect from most Greek men. He was not particularly tall but wore a big smile and a welcoming expression. He made us feel comfortable and at home.

"Come in, come in," Costas encouraged. "Please sit."

The restaurant was small, with tables and chairs like that of a pizza shop. It was not fancy, but it was nice.

"*Ti káneis* [how are you]?" my father offered in comfortable Greek.

Costas' expression changed, and he became more engaged when he realized we were Greek.

"*Kalá efcharistó* [good, thank you]," answered Costas.

A conversation in Greek ensued, the result of which was Costas bringing us his premiere menu selections—no menu or ordering necessary.

Some of us were slightly skeptical about "restaurant style" Greek food. After all, we each had our own discerning Greek palates and, back at home, there are two types of restaurants I prefer to avoid: Greek and Italian. The reason behind this snobbery is that the food never lives up to that prepared by my mother and grandmothers.

My family's Greek specialties include spanakopita (pita for short: spinach and feta pie), *pastitsio* (creamy noodles and ground lamb or beef), dolmades with *avgolemono* sauce (stuffed grape leaves with lemon egg sauce), *galaktoboureko* (custard and filo pie), baklava (honey, nut, and filo pastry), *kourabiedes* (butter cookies with powdered sugar), and, of course, a mouth-watering leg of lamb.

I don't usually eat any of these items outside of my family gatherings because I know I will judge them unfairly. But we were in Greece, so I decided to make an exception and give the food a try.

"Mom, what are the chances we don't like what we are about to eat?" I asked.

"Don't be silly. I'm sure it will be fine."

Mom said "fine" as if she too thought it might not be up to snuff.

We were pleasantly surprised to find that this Greek fare was every bit as delicious as any of our secret family recipes.

And, I daresay, in a different way than we were used to at home. Whatever variation in spices, ingredients, or home-grown Greek herbs used in Costas' recipes offered a refreshing take on the flavors our palates were used to.

The meal began with a tzatziki yogurt that I could have eaten by the bowlful. It was generously drizzled with olive oil that made every unctuous mouthful better than the last.

Salads were also exceptional, with a hunk of mouthwatering feta cheese the size and thickness of a deck of cards.

"Look at the size of that feta," I said. "That is the most beautiful thing I have ever seen." At home, I always pay a premium for imported feta, while in Greece, it was domestic and delicious.

"I'm going to devour that in about three bites," Karla added.

And she did. We were like kids in a candy shop, but to these Greek foodies, this food was better than any candy that ever hit our sweet tooth. We were in food heaven and barely coming up for air.

By the expressions on everyone's faces whenever they looked up from their plates long enough for me to see, I would say the Greek food in Greece was well received by all. As the main courses made their way to the table, I realized that I might want to catch my breath before round two. Generous plates of moussaka (Greek lasagna with eggplant), pita, stuffed peppers, *pastitsio*, and more were put down nanosecond before arms reached out to get ahold of what each of us wanted before it was gone.

We also enjoyed a bottle of wine that Costas gifted to Bob because Bob was celebrating his forty-sixth birthday. By this time, we were all happy, stuffed, and satisfied. Even Ally liked the bowl of plain spaghetti Costas so graciously served to my little lady with a picky palate. I think there were some French fries at the table, too. Ugh, you can take the kids out of America, but you can't blah, blah, blah, you know the rest.

"I don't think I can move, I'm so full," said Tony.

"Actually, I think moving around is exactly what we need to help us digest," I said.

"Oh, God, no, I need a nap! What are you thinking?"

"Shopping, of course! Trust me; it'll be good for us."

I couldn't possibly be in Athens and not find a something to take home as a remembrance.

Luckily, George told us that the local Plaka Flea Market was the best place to shop. Plaka is an old historical neighborhood in Athens nearby the Acropolis.

"Go here, it has a little bit of everything," he said.

This was the perfect contained outdoor shopping area where we could venture off and explore. In typical fashion, the men, including Alex, took off to some local bar. Apparently, though, the men were not entirely turned off by shopping, because Alex turned up in the end with his own little purchase of a mini mandolin or ukulele called a *bouzouki*.

I walked away with a leather handbag with a large floral print that reminds me of Greece every time I use it. I love that it is different and boldly colored—something that I like to equate with my Greek heritage. Karla purchased three silver pendants, each featuring the Greek key with a lovely blue stone set in the center. Like my Yia Yia and her gift of the Parthenon pendants, Karla gave one each to Katherine, Julia, and Ally. They are a precious reminder of our trip, their heritage, and their familial bond.

We had put in a full day, but as George shuttled us back to the ship, he surprised us with one final stop: a little Greek pastry shop. Karla purchased a small box of flaky bites of baklava and other Greek delicacies. One of them was so artfully designed that it reminded me of a bite-size bird's nest. We intended to save these yummy morsels for later, but they barely made it out of the shop.

Back on board the ship, we readied ourselves for the holy land of Ephesus, Turkey.

12. Pace Yourself

I KNOW MANY PEOPLE WHO'D TRAVEL EXCLUSIVELY by cruise ship if given the chance. The idea that so many wonderful things like activities, casinos, extravagant buffets, and the camaraderie of other passengers are within arm's reach is certainly appealing. At the same time, though, it makes overindulging much too easy.

If you're like me, you're not accustomed to constant touring, dining, and nearly continuous socializing. There comes a point when the entire experience becomes overwhelming.

This trip, however, had me caught up in all things new and exciting. I nearly forgot about my love for downtime until I found myself close to exhaustion. I needed to take a break but had such a hard time figuring out what would be okay to miss. Normally, I'm decisive to a fault, but here my FOMO (Fear Of Missing Out) was at an all-time high.

At home, I know whatever I'm choosing to skip out on will probably happen again in some shape or form. Life in suburbia is nothing if not redundant. But here, I didn't want to regret my decision to decline. Nearly everything we did was a once-in-a-lifetime experience.

Feeling so excited and optimistic about our Mediterranean journey made me realize, now more than ever, that the pre-trip anxiety I struggled with was such a waste of energy.

I was enjoying myself in the same way I did when I traveled in my twenties. The more I embraced the here and now, the more I knew the fear was something I had to let go of.

Following our day in Athens, I contemplated my renewed affection for travel over a nap, because after that excursion, I was spent beyond belief. More than ever, I realized how entirely overrated and unhealthy the go-go-go mentality of life at home was. I can't tell you the number of times Tony has said, "I feel guilty because I haven't done anything productive today." It's a Sunday, for God's sake. Take the day of rest! I'm a firm believer that it's good for the body and soul to do nothing—absolutely nothing. And so, after Athens, I slept.

Not typically a day sleeper, I felt like a new person upon rising. I already felt recharged and eager to take on our next scheduled stop in Turkey the next day. But before that, we had another delightful dinner aboard the ship and another full night of sleep.

"Mom, what are you wearing to dinner tonight?" asked Julia.

"I don't know, but I really wish it could be pajamas," I answered.

Despite my energizing nap, I could've used a night in.

I'd grown to both love and hate the idea of getting ready every night to go out for dinner. Whether we were in the ship's formal dining room or one of the low-key cafés, some degree of preparation was required. At the start, I loved picking through the dressy clothes I took such care in packing and deciding what I was in the mood to wear. But then it got old. Or maybe it was me feeling old. I missed my comfy clothes and going to bed by nine p.m. I could feel my happy, vacation mode shell starting to crack ever so slightly.

As hard as I tried to pace myself when it came to rest and responsible eating and drinking, I did run into a slight problem one evening when our aggressive touring schedule caught up with me.

Just before dinner, the evening prior to arriving in Turkey, I attempted to slip on a pair of heels, and a sharp pain shot up my right leg. It caught me by surprise, but I didn't give it too much attention. I swapped the shoes out for a low-heel and proceeded with some minor discomfort—nothing I couldn't handle.

I ignored the pain as long as possible and was honestly surprised when it continued to give me trouble. I had no recollection of injury, and there were no signs of swelling, bruising, or a bug bite, yet it hurt so much, I couldn't ignore it. The persistent pain was very odd, and I couldn't come up with any cause or a clear description.

"Are you limping?" asked Tony.

"Yeah, my leg is killing me."

"What did you do?"

"I honestly have no idea."

"What's it feel like?"

"I don't know, but it really friggin' hurts!"

Normally, I'd say I have a very high threshold for pain. I've twisted my ankle to the point where I've been lightheaded, and my foot turned black and blue, yet I've managed to keep on walking. But if the pain worsens and lingers, that's when I get panicky.

"Pop a few Advil and let's see how you feel after dinner," Tony said.

"Oh, okay, Dr. Tony, thanks for the advice."

That night I was happy to get off my feet. I assumed that a good night's rest would resolve the issue. But sometime after midnight, I awoke in agony. I tried to quietly deal with it by massaging the area and elevating my leg on a pillow. Elevation was not the way to go! As soon as I raised my leg, it caused the oddest sensation. The shooting pain oozed down my leg. I freaked out. It felt like whatever it was was slowly creeping its way toward the rest of my body. I jumped up and began shaking the pain back down to my foot where it had begun. Any desire to remain quiet was lost. I was loudly and disruptively flexing, stretching, and hopping around until I could finally stand still.

"What is going on?" Tony asked, waking up to my turmoil.

"It's my foot, the pain is so bad. I think I've got gout from all the eating and drinking."

I really don't know where that came from. I've been known to jump to outrageous conclusions when under duress.

"What are you talking about? It's not gout. Go see the ship's doctor."

Tony has no qualms about rushing to the ER at the slightest indication of medical concern. I avoid a trip to the doctor at all costs.

"No! It's the middle of the night; I don't want to go to any cruise ship doctor."

All I could think about was Doc on *The Love Boat*. With that in mind, I decided it was best if I just calmed down, took a few deep breaths, popped more Advil, and waited until morning.

Eventually the Advil kicked in and the pain subsided long enough for me to fall back to sleep. When I woke up, I was feeling better with some remaining but manageable discomfort.

"That was so bizarre," I said to Tony. "What the hell is the matter with me?"

"You know, it was probably those flimsy flip-flops you wore all day in Athens," he said. "You really should be wearing more sensible shoes."

"Great, thanks, now you tell me."

Not until Tony said it did it even occur to me that it was my shoes. I live in flip-flops during the summer months at home and never have a problem. Then again, I'm not trekking miles through the rocky terrain of the Acropolis. Rather than dwell on the issue any further, I determined that the flip-flop explanation was, indeed, the likely source of my problem. From then on, sneakers were my go-to shoe choice for all major touring expeditions. My shoe fetish aside, form over fashion would have been the wiser choice.

This minor run of bad luck was only temporarily off-putting; with just a little TLC over the next twenty-four hours, I was able to resume normal activity with no residual pain. Onward and upward; Turkey, here we come. But first, one more fancy dinner on-ship.

That night we celebrated Bobby's forty-sixth birthday and gathered in the formal dining room. I chose to have just one celebratory cocktail and opted for the light menu. I couldn't get the thought of gout out of my mind, as ridiculous as it was. I figured backing off the rich foods and copious cocktails couldn't hurt, at least for one night.

The formal dining room was something to behold. It spanned two levels. The focal point was an oversize wine tower with the dual purpose of impressing guests while holding the ship's two-thousand-bottle wine collection. When not admiring views of wines of the world, the glass elevators, and the blimp-size chandelier, we enjoyed pleasant conversation with our regular servers, wine sommelier, and bartender.

Each staff member, whether in the dining room or elsewhere on the ship, was friendly and engaging. They were thrilled to interact with us and talk about their lives and experiences traveling the world. I loved hearing about the various cultures and lifestyles, both on board the ship and off. Having the same servers each night was a wonderful way to develop a connection and comfort level, like you might at a favorite restaurant back home.

We did possibly get too close for comfort with one crew member.

One night, on our family trek from our cabins to the dining room, Bobby happened by two cabin attendants who didn't hear us coming. That's hard to believe with our boisterous bunch, but the two clearly had other things on their minds. Bobby caught a brief glimpse of the two men in what appeared to be an affectionate embrace just as he passed by. They were nestled in one of the alcoves leading into a cabin, so the rest of us never even noticed they were there. Bobby didn't think much of the situation. But later one of the two room attendants tracked him down and made a point to tell him that what he'd seen was not what it appeared to be.

"Sir, excuse me for the intrusion, but I must explain that what you saw earlier in the corridors wasn't what you might have thought," said the attendant.

"Oh sure, no problem," Bob answered. "No worries at all." His nervous, loud laughter drew our attention.

"It's just that I don't want a passenger to walk away with the wrong idea. I'm married with children, you understand?"

"Of course," said Bob. "Don't give it another thought— really."

All this caught Bob off guard. He'd forgotten about the two men in the halls until this young, seemingly guilt-stricken, man approached him about it.

This poor guy should have left well enough alone. The exchange between him and Bob was odd and totally unnecessary, since Bob could not have cared less either way.

"What was that all about?" Karla asked the moment Bob approached our table.

"Well, this is a first," Bob said as he went on to whisper the details of what had transpired.

"*Awk*-ward!" Alex inserted in that funny, drawn out way that teenagers do.

At the expense of the cabin attendant, we enjoyed the unexpected and juicy dinner conversation.

I can only imagine what else goes on below deck on these huge cruise ships.

A good meal, good company, and good gossip—we were ready for Turkey.

13. Turkey

BY THE TIME THE SHIP DOCKED IN TURKEY, WE were ready to step out again. While our sea days were meant to be restorative, this last one left me itching to get off and get moving. I function much more productively when I'm focused on things other than myself, and Turkey was about to have my full attention.

"Why are we only making one stop in Turkey?" I said to Tony. "I'm excited to see Ephesus, but what about Istanbul and Cappadocia?"

"You can't have it all. Ephesus is where the ship takes us, and that's all we have time for."

"It feels weird to be so close to some of these other places I'd love to see and not go there. Such a tease."

Ultimately, if you really want to sink your teeth into the culture of any one place, traveling by cruise just isn't the way to go. Cruising is much like a tasting party. At these trendy little shindigs, you sample various little bites of foods. You may enjoy one or many, but if you happen to relish one bite in particular, you are out of luck, because that's all there is. When you travel by cruise ship, you similarly get a flavor for the areas you visit, but if you want more, you'll have to come back another time for a full serving. In either case, just like I preach to my girls, you have to live the moment and savor what you have in front of you. So, no whining about what I couldn't see and a whole lot of anticipation for what I could.

My Mediterranean tasting party certainly stimulated my travel taste buds. We talked frequently about where we'd like to return. The more we saw, the more I felt each place deserved more time; I was being completely sucked into future travel by my own volition. As long as I didn't think about how I'd get there, I was rolling with the possibilities.

Turkey, more than any of our other stops, was exceptionally brief. Both because we saw only one very small part and because we had to spend part of the time dodging an unwelcome sales pitch.

We docked in Kusadasi, Turkey's major cruise port and a resort town, to explore the nearby Holy Land of Ephesus. We only had about eight hours until we were required to be back at the ship. It was excruciatingly hot, but we were all very interested in seeing this Biblical land with so much historical significance.

Ephesus reminded me of an epic colony of dilapidated sand castles. Everything that surrounded us had what appeared to be a sandy white coating. I imagined if I ran my hand across any surface, a chalky residue would remain on my palm and fingers. At one point my mother hugged one of the king-sized columns to get a sense of its size. Her little arms couldn't make their way around to meet. When she pulled away, I fully anticipated that she'd be covered in dust. She wasn't.

This allowed my fleeting mind to refocus on what was really important about the ancient city that stretched for miles in front of us: I began thinking about the people who had walked the dirt paths before us. I marveled at the importance of it all. Jesus' Apostles had been there; Cleopatra and Mark Antony had lived there, and Ephesus is also believed to be the final resting place of Mary, the mother of Jesus.

We saw her stone dwelling from a distance, at the top of Bulbul Mountain. It was hard to imagine I was standing in the same place where these prominent and powerful people once stood. I realized, in that moment, that so much of what is taught in the Bible, in Christianity, and in history books, can seem more like fairy-tales than actual historical events. Years of learning about and conceptualizing these larger-than-life figures made them seem more like characters in a play than people. Visiting Ephesus brought them to life.

When I say the spirit of the land came to life, it may sound melodramatic, but an overstatement it is not. At one point along our self-guided tour, an unexpected sound of loud music drew our attention away from the land.

"What in the world is going on over there?" I said.

Out of what seemed like nowhere appeared a large, costumed group of people dressed as Cleopatra, Mark Antony, and their entourage. Trumpets sounded, drums bellowed, and royal performers waved to the crowd.

"This couldn't have come at a better time," said Dad. "I need a breather."

I think we all did. We had walked quite a long way, and we took this opportunity to stop and sit on whatever rock or open patch of dusty earth was available.

We watched as Cleopatra's attendants, resplendent in white and gold, Grecian-style outfits, engaged in an Egyptian dance. I couldn't help but think of The Bangles "Walk Like an Egyptian," circa 1986.

Gladiators entered and took center stage. They launched into a grandiose sword fight. I was riveted and most appreciative of this break for the kids' sake. Seeing a live performance like this not only broke up the monotony of touring, but it allowed them to connect what they've learned in school to what they were witnessing right in front of them.

We all enjoyed the show, both for its entertainment value and its role as intermission to the much bigger show of legendary Ephesus itself. Like most of the historic, and some of the modern-day, architecture we'd seen thus far, Ephesus did not disappoint when it came to phenomenal examples of archaeological preservation. The Great Theater of Ephesus and the Library of Celsus were both exceptional. Just to walk by the theater was enough to make your jaw drop. Built into the slope of Panayir Hill, the theater's sixty-six rows of steep stone stands seemed to reach epic heights. We chose not to investigate the Great Theater but passed by from a distance. From this vantage point, the venue had a much bigger and more commanding appearance than the theaters we'd seen previously in Ostia Antica and Sicily.

We did enter the Library of Celsus and took time inside to meander and take it all in. The reconstructed facade of the building was beautifully intact. The tall structure features a wide set of stairs leading to the library's landing, on which four pairs of Corinthian columns separate the three entryways to the interior. At the second level, a repeating set of columns sit atop those on the bottom, and window openings occupy the spaces in between. It was easy to envision the scrolls and manuscripts once stored inside and the reading room the windows were intended to illuminate. It was quite magnificent.

Fully enriched by our walk through time and history, we decided to wrap up this leg of our day early. We made our way to the exit, moving through at a relatively quick pace while drafting the rest of the tourist pack.

This time, I found it was nice to walk through an ancient city without a tour guide to lead the way. It gave my mind time to wander and me the opportunity to stop and inspect the unusual things that I find interesting. Admittedly, without someone to keep us focused, we periodically got off track.

Enter the feral cats of Ephesus. While there was so much to see from times past, several of us were distracted by the living and breathing occupants of Ephesus. Hundreds of cat families had found homes in the nooks and crannies of the ruins. They were everywhere. Big ones and little ones alike walked comfortably alongside the sightseers without hesitation or concern. While most tourists passed by the furry creatures, we found ourselves focusing on them more than we should have. Karla must have pointed out, as she called them, "the baby kitties," at least a dozen times. We were clearly getting punchy.

"Auntie, it can't be both a baby and a kitty at the same time," Julia finally ridiculed sweetly. "It's just a kitty, and most of them are cats."

Karla didn't miss a beat.

"Oh no, Jujee," she said lovingly but emphatically. "Just look at them all, they're all just baby kitties."

I started laughing uncontrollably, which was our cue to go.

Throughout Ephesus, you could not escape the feeling of being thrown back in time. Then we reached the end of the lengthy biblical roads and were shockingly and conveniently dumped into a makeshift shopping plaza offering a plethora of wares from Turkish retailers. Suddenly, 2012 smacked us in the face.

Some might have been put off by the modern-day commercialism, which was intrusively placed at the end of such a significant location, but I'm no such shopping snob.

"Ooh, what's this? I didn't know this would be here," I said gleefully.

Suddenly every lady in the group perked up. I could hear Tony grumbling behind us.

Happy as we were to enjoy a little retail therapy, we were all taken aback by the sheer aggressiveness and audacity of the Turkish merchants. They bombarded us with brazen sales tactics, and this was just as we were passing by. If you so much as took a brief look at an item, you'd be accosted and pressured to buy it. At one point a salesman became upset with Karla when she asked a few questions then decided against purchasing an item. He was clearly insulted that she'd wasted his time.

Bob told us he'd been taken into some kind of tented backroom to view ancient coins. The seller said that because Bob was "his friend," he'd make him a special deal. Bob said he found it entertaining; I'd say it was scary.

"Why the hell would you go into some random backroom?" I said. "You're lucky you came back out."

Ally and Katherine were asked where their money was and when they answered, "with our moms," the shop owner told them to go get us.

It was so uncomfortable; I could barely stand it. Not so much that I didn't walk away with a beautiful Turkish plate and some other tchotchkes, but the whole scene had me feeling uneasy and on guard.

When I'd had all I could take of the pushy peddling, my mother and I snuck away from the madness and took some time to reflect as the rest of our crew continued to browse the market.

Ahead of us were Julia and Katherine enjoying a little time together.

My mother commented on how tall Julia was compared to Katherine, who's almost two years older.

She paused and then she said it—the phrase that is humorously burned in my memory like branding on cattle.

"Look at them, Beth," she said. "Julia is already so tall, and she hasn't even started her menses."

What did she just say? Menses? The word hit me like a brick, and I fixated on it as soon as I heard it. Now there's a term that seemed as old as the archaic grounds we were walking on, and I couldn't help but giggle to myself. Who says menses anymore? The more I thought about it, the funnier I thought it was. I couldn't keep this funny nugget to myself; I had to share it with someone. Who better, or possibly worse, than my sister?

As soon as I recounted the conversation, the word menses took on a whole other level of funny. Like me, Karla questioned, "Menses?" except she said it out loud while laughing uproariously. We couldn't help it. In all that heat and seriousness of Ephesus, suddenly the word menses just sounded side splittingly funny.

Like all good laughs, we didn't want to let this one go, so we managed to hold on to it throughout the trip. Whether appropriate or not, Karla and I found every opportunity to work the word "menses" into any conversation.

If I said my shoulder hurt, Karla would say, "I wonder if it might be your menses?" If someone looked at us funny, we'd say, "They must be on their menses." It really didn't matter what the situation was, menses made it funnier every single time. It never got old. Except, I'm sure, to my mother.

"For heaven's sake, girls, I have no idea why you think that word is so funny," she said.

After the menses joke had pretty much been beaten to a pulp, I finally asked my mother, "Mom, why didn't you just say period?"

"We were in a crowd of people," Mom answered. "I didn't want to sound crude."

Here Mom was trying to be proper and polite, and my sister and I made a small scene snickering and laughing like silly schoolgirls.

Our day in Ephesus ended in pure exhaustion. The driver we had arranged to get us there picked us up, and all we wanted to do was head back to the ship.

Turns out, he had other ideas. The driver, like the Turkish salesmen in the bazaar, was insistent, to say the least. To our dismay, he was thoroughly preoccupied with our day ending in a trip back to his family's hotel, where he promised us the chance to view and purchase handcrafted Turkish rugs. We had no interest in any further activity, much less a viewing of Turkish rugs. Thank God for Tony, who graciously did the dirty work for our weary group and told the man that we were done for the day and needed to return to the boat.

But, man, this guy would not take no for an answer. He kept pushing and pushing—he wouldn't let it go. It was so uncomfortable because I hate being badgered and especially because he was the one behind the wheel. I began to worry that he would ignore our wishes and hijack us to his hotel.

Thankfully the Daigle–Kittler–Thomas clan is a scrappy bunch, and we would not give in. If he hadn't acquiesced to our request when he did, there was a very good chance that my hot Greek and Italian temper would have boiled over. I'm glad I didn't end up yelling at this man, even though I felt like he deserved it. We were boat-bound and ready for another relaxing night and day at sea.

14. Downtime

IF SOMEONE HAD TOLD ME THAT ON DAY TEN AWAY
from home I'd be completely relaxed and unconcerned about
what I might be missing, I'd have said they didn't know me
at all. But maybe a new me was emerging, because home was
the last thing on my mind. I was in the midst of fully embracing and understanding the value of the present.

A book I like to read around the holidays, *The Precious
Present* by Spencer Johnson, M.D., talks about valuing the
moment you are in or else you will gain nothing from it. I
was in that state of mind and hoped it would stay with me
permanently.

We had intentionally cut our touring time in Turkey short.
Since most of the ship's passengers were still in port, we had
the boat practically to ourselves. An entire afternoon aboard
a nearly desolate Equinox to do with as we pleased. We kept
it simple and chose to putter around and check out aspects of
the ship we'd yet to take advantage of. I had already sworn off
the pool and received as many spa services as a not-so-high-
maintenance diva could take. We were left with sunbathing,
napping, or the ship's movie theater.

"Kids, I'm all yours," I said. "What do you want to do for
the afternoon?"

"We're swimming, then going to a cupcake-making work-shop, and then we are meeting Noni to play bingo," said Katherine.

Cupcake-making workshop and bingo—who knew?

"Who's we?" I asked.

"Me, Julia, and Ally," said Katherine.

"Yeah, see you later, Mom," Julia said with a wave as she and Ally walked off.

Well, it seemed my stealthy plan to loosen the apron strings had worked out.

If that wasn't a sign to take a little time for myself, I don't know what was. Part of me was surprised and a little caught off guard that my girls had planned the rest of their day without me, but I quickly shook that off and began thinking about what I would do with my free time.

I didn't bother to ask Tony and Bob what they were up to because I knew they'd end up at the casino one way or another. I also knew where my dad was headed without question: back to his cabin for a nap.

Karla and I decided this would be the perfect chance to take in one of the on-ship movies. It wouldn't be crowded and the likelihood of staying awake was pretty good, seeing it was only around three in the afternoon.

"I haven't been to a movie theater in years," I said to Karla.

"Why not?" Karla asked.

"I'm too tired at night. It's easier and more comfortable to sit on my own couch."

"That's lame."

She was right, but I'd fallen victim to becoming one of those mothers who makes little time for herself. I put that on the list of things to change as the new me.

The ship's theater was nice. It featured wall-to-wall carpet, comfy seats, and an air of understated elegance that was unexpectedly inviting. The ambiance made the simple outing feel more like a luxury. *The Girl with the Dragon Tattoo* was playing, and I was intrigued. I hadn't seen it or read the book but knew about the hype surrounding the film at the time of its release. I thought it would be worth watching. Karla had read the book and agreed. I would like to think that my older sister might have given me adequate forewarning of the extreme intensity of this story, but instead, she loosely mentioned that it was disturbing.

This description was in no way sufficient. Seeing that I find walking around my neighborhood at dusk to be "disturbing," I had no clear understanding of exactly what Karla was suggesting. I went into the flick having no idea what I was about to see.

We entered the quiet theater to find we were the only ones there. Karla and I took our seats and waited for the show to begin. Before the movie even began, a heavyset man with gray hair and a beard, maybe in his sixties, walked in. He scanned the theater with all but the two seats Karla and I were in unoccupied, and then plopped himself right the hell next to me. I nearly gasped at his audacity. There was no courtesy seat between us, just the narrow armrest that I was now expected to share with this space-invading stranger.

For the love of all that is moderately normal in this world, the room was full of empty seats. Why would this man choose to cross the line of personal space so egregiously? This complete infraction of spatial appropriateness was so far beyond my comfort zone that I reacted physically. My heart raced, and my palms grew sweaty. There was no way I could sit through the whole movie this way.

The lights were dim, this guy was kind of creepy, and, like in any movie theater, the seats were much closer than any normal person would like them to be, even if seated beside people they love. Good God, I thought, really?

I exchanged several horrified glances with my sister. I needed to make a move and quick. In a moment of panicked brilliance, I stood up and loudly announced to Karla, "Hey, I need to use the ladies' room before the show starts, how about you?"

"Oh yeah, good idea," she replied. I assumed Karla understood that I wouldn't normally broadcast my restroom requirements for all to hear, but we were in a predicament that necessitated bold tactics.

We entered the bathroom, neither of us having to use it, and burst out laughing at the insanity of it all.

"Who in their right mind would do that?" I asked.

"Clearly someone without proximity issues," Karla said. "What do we do now?"

"We've got to sit someplace else. It's just too weird. This guy clearly has no boundaries. I can't go back to the same seat and be uncomfortable for two hours."

"This would be so much easier if he weren't the only other person in there," Karla said. "It's going to be so awkward."

"We are already so far past awkward," I said. "Come on, and whatever you do, don't make eye contact."

In that moment, I felt like we were Lucy and Ethel trying to get ourselves out of a tricky situation. Upon our return, we went ahead and unapologetically chose other seats several rows back. This kept us out of his sight and him in ours—right where I could keep an eye on him.

What I would soon learn while watching *The Girl with the Dragon Tattoo* was that this guy was the least of my worries. The movie itself managed to eviscerate every last bit of tranquility in my body.

I honestly considered walking out. Why do filmmakers put such vile content on screen? And what about the book's author? How did he come up with this dreadful story? It was far too violent and sexually explicit for my taste, and despite its popularity, I felt worse off for having seen it.

I hate to sound simple, but my idea of entertainment is something joyful or funny. I recognize that people enjoy different things, but I feel certain stories take things too far. For me, *The Girl with the Dragon Tattoo* was one of them.

Even as a kid, I couldn't handle scary television.

One of my earliest memories, from when I was seven or eight, is of being frozen under my sheets after watching *The Wizard of Oz*. I was so frightened and convinced that the evil witch was in my room. How I wished I had watched a lighthearted episode of *The Brady Bunch* or *The Electric Company* instead.

I'm just a silly sitcom kind of girl who appreciates getting lost in the stupidity and humor of lighthearted programs. Yes, *The Real Housewives* makes my cut, and for that I'm not proud but also not ashamed. I admit that reality TV is my guiltiest pleasure. These shows are my therapy. I need them to decompress, and seeing that they are all mind-numbingly idiotic, it works out very well. They are like my own form of mindless meditation. There were times on this cruise that I desperately wished for a little TV downtime, but we didn't want to hang out in our rooms even to watch TV.

Too bad *Bridesmaids* or *Horrible Bosses* hadn't been on the ship's marquee. Now those are the kinds of silly movies I can at least sit through with a smile.

While our on-ship movie left my mind racing, I was still happy to have done something I normally wouldn't.

"So, what did you think?" Karla asked as we walked out of the theater.

"I'm traumatized."

"I told you it was disturbing."

"Right, disturbing has a whole new meaning to me now."

We walked away, and as if on autopilot, found ourselves headed toward the ship's shops. Just what my frazzled nerves needed. My mind was quickly redirected to a happy place as we made our way to peruse the on-ship wares.

Who'd have guessed that a quiet afternoon on board the desolate ship would turn out to be so eventful?

Meanwhile, I would later learn that while Karla and I were inside the theater, the rest of our family had gathered on the pool deck where a belly dancing performance was underway.

"Beth, too bad you missed the belly dancer," my mom said. "You would have gotten a hoot out of it."

"Why?" I asked. "Was there something funny about it?"

"Well, sort of," said Mom. "The dancer had an eye for your husband, so she dragged him up to dance with her."

"Oh, really?" I said. So, while Karla and I had been busy ditching a creeper in the movie theater, Tony was twirling around with a sexy belly dancer.

"He busted out his 'sprinkler' and 'lawnmower' moves," said Bob.

"The poor belly dancer."

15. The Greek Islands

The Winding Roads of Rhodes

We were now preparing for the glorious islands of Greece. Our three island destinations would give us a different perspective than we had in Athens, and we were anxious to explore each one.

Rhodes was our first stop. The families decided to break up and do their own things. The Kittlers rose bright and early to head off onto the island, while Mom and Dad decided to stay close to the ship. Up to this point, I really hadn't been alone with just Tony, Julia, and Ally, and I was looking forward to a little private time with my peeps.

"Ladies," Tony called that morning before we'd even changed out of our pajamas, "what should we do today?"

I was so happy not to have to rush out for a tour or another scheduled activity.

"Room service!" the girls answered excitedly.

It's funny how something like room service can be the highlight of a kid's vacation. We enjoyed a slow morning over eggs, bacon, and several wonderful cups of coffee. By the time we disembarked, the gangway was clear, and we were energized for whatever might come our way.

We had no tour guides to direct us in the Greek Islands. We were content to operate independently and hoped that all Tony's planning would pay off.

We were unambitious in Rhodes. We aimed to walk about the town, do some shopping, and end our time with our first delightful dip into the Mediterranean, where we planned to meet up with the Kittlers on the beach.

"It's nice to be together, just the four of us, don't you think?" I asked, angling to be told what I wanted to hear.

"Yeah, it's good, but when are we going to see Alex and Katherine?" asked Julia.

"Really? You're lucky you aren't sick of each other yet."

"Mom, we'll never get sick of each other," said Ally. "We're family."

That was cute. If she only knew how many families don't get along.

As much as I wanted Julia and Ally to myself, I wasn't surprised that they were anxious for peer interaction so quickly. At home, our free time is often spent in group activities surrounded by friends, neighbors, and members of our community. We are lucky to have people in our lives with whom we enjoy spending time, but it also chips away at precious time with our own family unit. As the four of us made our way through Rhodes, I made a point to burn each moment we spent there a little deeper into my memory.

The city of Rhodes on the Island of Rhodes was a neat, rather urban place that had a little bit of everything.

Our first unexpected happenstance, as we strolled along stone pathways, was our viewing of Roloi, the Clock Tower. We also stumbled upon the Palace of the Grand Master of the

Knights of Rhodes (aka Kastello) where the Grand Master resided and the Order of Knights assembled.

The Clock Tower was an eye-catching sight, both for its Byzantine style and the erected suits of armor that flanked either side of it. It is said to have been originally built at the end of the seventh century. Since that time, it was reconstructed twice. Once after being nearly destroyed in an explosion, and then again after having been neglected over a one-hundred-and-fifty-year time period. Today, it is a striking landmark that I was compelled to photograph from as many angles as I could. If so inclined, visitors can climb the deep wooden steps to the top of the tower to take in the beautiful views of Rhodes. We, however, didn't make that trek.

"Girls, stand over there so I can get a shot of you with the knight in the background."

"Mom, not again. Stop taking so many pictures."

"Why don't you kids ever want your picture taken?" I asked rhetorically. "Don't you want to capture these memories?"

"*No!*" both Ally and Julia shouted.

Kids are so rude.

Just beyond the Clock Tower was the Palace of the Grand Masters. I didn't expect to see a medieval castle on a Greek Island and was curious what this structure was all about.

"Should we go in?" Tony asked.

"Why not?" I said. "We have no other plans."

"Sure, it looks kinda cool," the girls agreed.

I was in shock—a positive and mutual response by all. I urged everyone forward before anyone could change their mind.

Inside, we learned that the palace was first constructed as a fort to defend against attacks should the outer wall of

Rhodes be breached. Later, following a takeover by the Turks in 1522 and an explosion in 1856, the building was rebuilt by Italians to become the summer residence of the notorious fascist dictator, Benito Mussolini.

The history lesson was a bit heavy for the girls, but we were all entranced by the extreme scale of this particular piece of architecture. The quiet, unencumbered halls were mysterious and made me wish they could talk. There were few other visitors at the time we were there, which made our jaunt through even more pleasurable, if not a little eerie. The sparsely filled, dimly lit rooms contained oversize furnishings (wardrobes, settees, and trunks) along with opulent ceiling-to-floor paintings.

I couldn't escape the feeling that we were on some kind of movie set fully equipped with large, cartoon-like wooden doors, turrets, and cannonballs. It was a stop worth making as it added substance to what was otherwise intended to be a relaxing shopping and beach day.

We meandered away from the historical sight and landed fortuitously upon the winding roads of Old Town Rhodes, where shopping was abundant and decidedly diverse. Inside the still-standing stone wall that surrounds Rhodes, there are many small streets lined with quaint shops. The girls and I were in our glory. Tony happily joined along as he people-watched outside the doorways of every shop we entered. Rhodes was very low-key. I didn't get the same "herd" feeling as I did in some of the other places we'd visited, and we all enjoyed the slower pace.

"There's something really fascinating about this island," Tony said. "I could see us coming back here."

I agreed, but oddly, out of all the Greek Islands, Rhodes was the one I knew the least about and had the lowest expectations for. A pleasant surprise.

Our time in Rhodes ended with a refreshing stop at Elli Beach.

"I can't wait to get in the water," said Julia.

"Me too," said Ally. "This is going to be the best part of the day."

TripAdvisor wasn't kidding when it said that Elli Beach was the most popular. I'd never seen a beach so packed. People were jammed onto every available inch of sand. Thankfully my normal crowd aversion didn't kick in. I was so intrigued by being a part of this "it" place that all else was forgotten.

As we scoped out lounge chairs, provided for a small fee, and scanned the gorgeous water, our eyes stopped at a perplexing visual obstruction. A short distance from shore, in the middle of the water, was an odd-looking structure that appeared to be a diving platform. Bathing suit-clad beauties, both male and female, were hanging out on this recreational apparatus turned flirt-fest that rose up from the water's surface like an iceberg. While it would appear that the purpose of the twenty-foot platform was to get some thrills by jumping from the top, young Rhodians and ambitious tourists seemed to have other ideas. The diving platform was not like typical diving boards you'd see at a pool. Access to the top landing was gained by an actual set of stairs versus a ladder. Handrails on either side of the steps kept jumpers headed straight to the top rather than launching off from the sides. It was the most bizarre idea of a diving board I'd ever seen. Most of the young people out there weren't diving or jumping at all; rather, they were using it as a meeting place to hang out away from the crowds.

The next thing I knew, Tony and Julia were on their way out to the water, saying they wanted to give it a try.

"Are you crazy?" I said. "I don't want Julia jumping off that thing."

To that, I got the cursory eye-roll, accompanied by, "Mom, it's fine. Don't be such a worry-wart."

Ally and I hung out on shore to take pictures.

"They are totally nuts if they go off that thing," Ally said.

I took comfort knowing I was not alone in my thoughts.

I watched closely as both Julia and Tony climbed the stairs and cautiously approached the edge of the platform. They both hesitated and peeked over the edge to get a better look at the challenge in front of them. Their body language suggested that they were second-guessing the leap.

I gasped when they jumped. It seemed their legs and arms were flailing forever. It was only a few seconds down to the salty water, but I imagined the jump felt much longer to them. To be at the top of that thing must have been far more frightening than anything we could've imagined from shore. I was impressed.

Upon their return, Tony whispered, "Holy crap, that was really high."

I enjoyed my own normal dip into the waters of Rhodes, and it felt like every impurity in my body was washed away in an instant. While I swam, Tony and the girls inspected the pebbled edge of the beach for unusual stones.

The salt water made me buoyant, so much so that I floated around in the wonderfully warm water in no rush to get out.

I'm usually a quick-dip kind of gal, but this was no icy, toe-numbing water like what I'm used to in New Hampshire and Maine. This was pure heaven. I relaxed and enjoyed every minute.

Despite the bustling beach, the tranquility of the Mediterranean was unsurpassed. I was convinced that the salty water held healing properties. Following my lengthy therapeutic swim, any lingering aches and pains from my flip-flop foot fiasco or sleeping in an unfamiliar bed disappeared.

I wish I had tolerance for swimming in the cold water at home so that I could spend more time in the ocean. My memory of my Yia Yia and her sister, Stella, treading water for nearly an hour in the frosty Ogunquit, Maine, water is so vivid. I can only wonder how they stood it. Without even a flinch of hesitation, Yia Yia would elegantly drift into the frigid water and swim about with a look of total pleasure.

"Girls," she would beckon while effortlessly treading water, "Come in! It's as warm as toast." She made it look so inviting, but even then, I needed time to adjust before fully submerging, and often, I never made it past my knees.

In Rhodes, I could channel my Yia Yia's love for the water without any thought whatsoever about the temperature. Elli Beach was perfection.

Our day in Rhodes was a nice break from all the familial togetherness. And it turned out, the break also afforded us a nice little reunion with the rest of our family when we all reconnected on the ship.

We learned that the Kittlers had walked around Old Town of Rhodes as well and had spent time watching a carpet maker weave a magnificent rug one strand at a time. They had been on Elli Beach at the same time as we were, but not surprisingly, we didn't run into each other.

The first thing out of Karla's mouth was, "Did you see that ridiculous deathtrap out in the middle of the water? You would have to be crazy to jump off that thing!"

"Call your niece and brother-in-law crazy, then."

She looked at me, horrified, and said, "Are you kidding me? That thing was clearly not OSHA approved—never in a million years!"

The Greek Islands were full of surprises.

Spectacular Santorini

Snow-capped mountains don't ordinarily come to mind when envisioning Greek Islands. Yet, they are exactly what I thought of when I first set eyes on Santorini. From a distance, the cluster of low-lying, whitewashed buildings, perched high atop the island, looked exactly like the snow-covered mountains of New Hampshire.

The way the little buildings on Santorini crept fluidly down the sides of the sloping land resembled a cappuccino mug overflowing with foamy white froth. The surreal sight came clearly into focus as the cruise ship neared the island.

"That's unbelievable," I said as we all stared at the magnificent topography. I was glad I hadn't googled this sight prior to the first time seeing it. Not knowing what to expect made it even more impressive.

"It really is," Tony agreed.

The beauty of the white pumice stone homes, businesses, and churches, built on and into Santorini's volcanic rock cliffs, was unlike anything that I'd seen before. This visual, backed by the lightly clouded, blue sky and the deep, turquoise waters beneath, was beyond picturesque.

We boarded the tender that would take us from the anchored cruise ship to the island. Exploring the island would have to wait, as most of our group would go right from the tender to a large wooden sailboat.

"What is it that you people are doing this morning?" asked my father.

He says, "you people" like we're a bunch of strangers.

"We already told you this. We are hiking up to the top of Santorini's volcano," Karla said.

"What?" Dad said, sounding shocked. "Why would you want to do that? Your mother and I aren't doing that, are we?"

"No, Dad, you and Mom are going to Santorini's main town," Karla said. "We thought the volcano might be something different for the kids."

"Okay, good, they can tell me all about it later, and I'll explain to them how volcanoes really work."

A teacher never rests.

Everyone but my parents set off to hike up the still-active volcano. We knew in advance that this might be too strenuous for them, so my mother made the executive decision to opt out on behalf of my father. While we did mention it to Dad in advance, he chose to ignore it until the moment it was happening. My parents had their own fun day planned and went directly to Santorini's famous village of Oia for a wine tour. I was sad to miss that, but figured the kids would appreciate the volcano far more than a wine tour.

The hike was a fun deviation from the usual sightseeing. We were ready for something other than shopping and ruins tours.

"I'm really looking forward to this," I said to Tony.

"Really? I wasn't sure you would like it."

"I know, but what are the chances I'll ever get to walk along an active volcano again?" I said.

Our volcano trek began on a sailboat that looked like something out of a pirate movie. It was constructed of glossy mahogany wood and had a massive mast. The allure of our transport boat made our short voyage to the volcano almost as eventful as the volcano itself. Not only because of the distinctive character of the boat, but because the crew were quite captivating.

The captain and his first mate were everything I would expect young Greek men to be. They had black, shiny hair slicked back to show off their dark olive skin and scruffy five o'clock shadows. They reminded me of many a Greek boy I saw at church when I was young.

Tony and Bob's boat experience was enhanced when they discovered that these business-savvy crewmen were selling Greek beer on board.

"Boys, don't feel like you have to partake in all of the onboard refreshments," I jibed.

"We don't want to seem rude," Bob said with a smile. "It's the least we can do to take advantage of what's being offered."

"Oh sure," I said, "you and Tony are nothing if not gracious guests."

As we approached the cove near the volcano, all we could see were boulder-size, charcoal-colored chunks of volcanic ash. The entire area appeared lifeless, yet there was a beauty to it. Like the symmetry of the white washed buildings atop Santorini, the pure, dark, monochromatic nature of what was before us seemed consistent and attractive in its own right.

Our guide on the volcano was a knowledgeable woman who told us everything about the history and science behind Santorini's volcano. I found this unexpectedly interesting and remained engaged throughout the entire tour. Santorini is one of the Cyclades islands of the Aegean Sea whose shape and form today is a result of a massive volcanic eruption in the sixteenth century. I'm not sure that the kids were as enthused with the educational component, but they seemed to appreciate that we were standing on a volcano and chatted happily among themselves.

"Wait till I tell my friends that I was on top of a volcano," Alex said.

"I don't really get how this is a volcano," Ally said. "It doesn't look like any volcano I've ever seen."

"That's because anything you've seen is on TV and erupting with lava and fire," Julia said. "This one isn't going to erupt."

"But it could," added Katherine. "The guide said it's still active."

"Wait, what?" said Ally, wide-eyed. She was obviously not listening to the presentation. Rather, she spent her time leaving her mark on the land.

All along the walking path atop the volcano were stone piles called "cairns," slightly reminiscent of the rock formations from *The Blair Witch Project*. These creations were left by previous visitors as messages to the Gods. It was clearly a thing, because they were everywhere. Not one to miss out on a growing trend, Ally created her own stack.

Meanwhile, Alex took a moment alone to sit along the volcano's slope. He peered out on the wondrous views that surrounded us and seemed to be deep in thought. I wondered what he was thinking about.

In a more interactive moment, we were all given the chance to see and feel the volcano's steam as it escaped from a small gap in the earth's surface.

"Everyone, gather around here," our guide instructed as she stood atop a large rock. "Behold the life of this volcano."

She motioned downward with her hand and there, sneaking out of a small patch of dirt, was a cloud of vapor.

"Place your hand above the haze and feel the volcano's heat," she said.

It was hard to believe that I was feeling the heat of a potential eruption. My hand was warm and damp when I pulled it away, and I felt an unexpected chill come over me.

We wandered on our own for a short while, taking in the incredible views before descending. Standing at the high point of the volcano, looking out at the tranquil Aegean Sea, there was nothing but water and islands all around us. It was peaceful. As I enjoyed that moment of calm, I realized that Alex must have been doing the same. The Mediterranean was making its mark on each of us.

The good vibes continued as we moved on to the next part of the volcano experience, a stop at Santorini's sulfur springs.

These springs are in shallow water near the volcanic islands and are believed to have therapeutic qualities. Our Viking sailboat was anchored a good distance away from the cove where the hot springs were located. To get there, we would all have to swim a short distance. The muddy appearance of the spring made me hope it would be worth the effort.

As we swam from the cool water where the boat was anchored to the warm, bath-like water of the spring, I couldn't help but think it was rather peculiar. What exactly had we just gotten into? To add to the perplexity, I noticed that the water was a murky reddish color. I was a little wigged out by this and the fact that I could see nothing below the surface. The lingering but not overpowering sulfur smell, like rotten eggs, wasn't helping.

"Yeesh," I said to Tony, "I hate that I can't see my hands under the water."

"I know," he said. "Anything could be swimming right beneath us."

"Oh God, I wish you hadn't said that."

A rush of uneasiness swept over me. I treaded water just long enough, by my estimation, to benefit from whatever cleansing qualities the spring had to offer.

"Look at those people over there," Karla said, eyeing some people near the shore. "They're slathering themselves with handfuls of mud."

Maybe they knew something that we didn't, but I had reached my sulfur limit. I just couldn't be sure that swimming in this stuff wasn't doing more harm than good.

Afterward, I didn't notice anything particularly positive or negative from the spring other than the slightly reddish tinge that remained on my bathing suit.

Our short sail back to the main island afforded us time in the wind and sun to dry off and catch our breath. Back at the island's docking area, we prepared to make our way up the side of the main island and up to the top of Santorini. Then bam! Reality hit.

"Oh no," I groaned. "Don't tell me that's the line to get to the top."

A slew of tourists, anxiously awaiting the same Greek Island experience as we were, were sweating the time away as they waited for cable car transportation from the bottom of the island to the top.

There were only two ways to the top: a long, steep walk or a questionable-looking gondola ride straight up the slope.

Tony mentioned that we could also ride our way up on the back of a donkey. I burst out laughing at the mere suggestion and placed myself firmly in line for the gondola.

The wait was about thirty minutes and was entirely worth it, but this would not be the last line we would stand in. This gorgeous little island, so perfect from a distance, was overrun with tourists.

From the gondola, we entered the town of Fira. This popular, high-traffic spot offers amazing views and plenty to do. We aimed to make our way to Oia Village, where the pace was said to be a bit slower and attractions like the Maritime Museum were located. But time and energy eluded us. We remained in Fira for the duration of the day.

I can easily imagine a week-long trip to Santorini to take in the villages, towns, and beaches we missed. We window-shopped, enjoyed a delicious meal, and absorbed the island atmosphere and its unmatchable views.

The most incredible ones came when we broke for lunch and enjoyed a solid stretch of time on the deck of a restaurant called Stani Tavern. It was billed as a sunset- and volcano-view tavern, and that it was. We were lucky, among such crowds, to have found a place that could accommodate eight of us with outdoor seating. The ocean view was amazing, and I could only imagine being there at dusk as the languid Mediterranean sun was setting.

In addition to the ocean, we gazed out onto distant islands, sloping cliffs that trickled with Santorini's signature white buildings, and hilltops that seemed to stretch to the heavens.

Following another excellent meal of Greek delicacies, we were fully fueled and ready to make our way back to the ship.

It was about this time that Tony's herd aversion presented itself in a rather literal way. Tony, Julia, Ally, Alex, and I all decided to return to the tender on foot. We thought walking down Santorini's slope would be manageable, and we had no interest in waiting for the gondola. The line to get down was triple what it was when we had arrived, and the donkeys still weren't happening. Or were they?

It turned out that the footpath and the donkey path were one and the same. As we approached it, happy that we weren't in the gondola line, we were faced with a sizable herd of donkeys all awaiting their descent.

"Oh my God, Mom," Julia said. "I have never seen so many donkeys. What are we going to do?"

There were at least one hundred agitated donkeys crammed into a small section of the path, and they had nowhere to go. Their handlers were doing their best to keep them calm, but they were all pushing each other and anyone who got in their way. I had no idea what the holdup was, but I knew someone had better make a move, and fast, or these poor beasts were going to lose it.

"This doesn't look good," I said to Julia. "There's no way we can pass until some of these donkeys move out."

We were stuck. To make matters worse, the donkey stench was disgusting.

"It's terrible that such a beautiful island could be so over-commercialized that something like this could happen," I said to Tony.

"I'm at a total loss for words right now," is all Tony could say as he gaped, repulsed, at the horde of asses before him.

Bottlenecked donkeys and permeating poop were not how I'd imagined Santorini. Despite the confusion, we did end up making it past the donkey station in about fifteen minutes, but those fifteen minutes seemed like an eternity.

Once past the animals, I thought we were in the clear. Spatially, we were no longer obstructed and were able to move briskly. However, we were reminded every step of the way that the donkeys owned this path. Donkey dung littered the trail at every turn.

"The smell is so bad I think I might puke," said Alex, while pinching his nose.

"I'm guessing the line for the gondola isn't looking so bad right about now, huh?" I said.

Eventually, we all made it down in one piece and lived to rehash our exit strategy from Santorini Island. We learned that Katherine and Bob attempted to ride the donkeys down.

"Are you serious?" I said to Karla. "You thought jumping off that diving board was bad, and you let your daughter get on the back of an angry ass?"

As it turned out, Katherine's kind heart couldn't bear to see the donkeys' struggle, so she abandoned the idea at the start before even attempting to mount one. My guess is that

Bob's super-sensitive gag reflex and the chaotic overcrowding of donkeys had something to do with it, too.

That evening, Katherine once again showed her pluck by rallying our troops to come together for one of the ship's youth activities: the kids' talent night. I strongly debated this plan, having been to enough school talent shows to know that this would likely be a painstaking endeavor.

But the fact that coordinating their on-ship performance took up all the kids' time that afternoon was a nice reprieve. The rehearsal for our youths' performance took place in our cabin, and while Katherine and Ally would be the only ones to perform, Alex and Julia made their contributions as choreographer (Julia) and audience critic (Alex).

I must admit that watching them together, so committed to their act and having so much fun in the process, made sitting through the show later that night entirely worth it. Katherine and Ally bonded over their flair for the arts, and Julia and Alex bonded over their silly monkey business off to the side.

Even when those two were all dressed up at formal cruise dinners, they were hooting and hollering with laughter over the most inane things. Whether Julia was spinning a cocktail umbrella in her mouth at the dinner table or Alex was cracking one of many mildly inappropriate jokes, the two of them were in a fit of giggles ninety percent of the time. The laughter was often contagious, except for those times they took it too far, and then it was annoying.

Ally and Katherine wowed the crowd at the talent show as they danced together "Dance Moms" style, and Katherine sang a beautiful solo of one of my favorite songs, "Don't Stop Believin'" by Journey.

I was impressed.

Mellow Mykonos

A good vacation must ebb and flow. Too many busy days make it feel like a rat race. Too many slow days may leave you feeling bored. Our time at sea generally took care of the ebb, but after our full day in Santorini, we were back out again to explore Mykonos the very next day. We planned a subdued beach day in Mykonos to keep things adequately chill.

Sleepy little Mykonos captured what one might expect from a Greek Island. It was not as modernized or commercialized as the other islands, and I found this inviting. Our cab driver took us to our one and only beach destination for the day, aptly named Paradise Beach.

During the fifteen-minute ride from the boat, we gazed out onto small white-and-blue homes sweetly set along the sides of the roads.

"Have you noticed the homes on the hillsides?" I asked Tony.

"Yeah, what about them?" he responded.

"I don't know; there's something so cute about them. Can you imagine such a small cluster like that being your entire community?"

The homes we were seeing were very small. Unlike the buildings atop Santorini, these structures had distance between them. They were not on top of each other, yet it was clear that each grouping was part of one village.

Every so often I would notice one building that stood out from the rest. They were churches, discreetly marked by a domed top or a steeple. The telltale sign that the buildings were churches was the barely visible cross that I could see only if the driver was passing ever so slowly.

"I bet living there would be peaceful," I commented.

"You'd be bored," Tony said.

"No, I wouldn't. Oh, I probably would, but the simplicity of it seems nice."

As we continued our way, my mind snapped back to what was happening inside the vehicle—namely, with our handsome Greek cab driver. He was everything that a sexy Greek man is cracked up to be. He reminded me of John Stamos, but with more of Greek God-like presence. His long, curly dark locks and beautiful Greek accent took his natural good looks to a superlative level.

His name was Dimitri, and when he spoke, his words were fluid and soothing.

"Hello, where can I take you today?" he asked.

"Paradise Beach," Tony answered quickly, not realizing that I was gawking.

"Very good," our driver said. "It's a perfect day for the scenic route; may I take you that way?"

How adorable, I thought. I was completely caught up in his style, accent, and sweet demeanor. Any other cabbie would take us for an extended ride intentionally to up the fare, but this man asked permission. Permission granted!

Accents are my weakness. I'm sure to find any person with an accent of any kind at least ten times more attractive than I would if they didn't have one.

"Do you think people from other countries think our accent is beautiful?" Julia once asked me.

"No," I said a little too abruptly.

"Why not?" she persisted.

"There's just something musical about a French, Italian, or Greek accent. You know what I mean?"

Living in America might be "living the dream," but one of the things we lack is a gorgeous accent.

We reached our Paradise Beach destination and bid adieu, or better yet, *adio* in Greek, to our handsome driver. We were again on our own as Tony, the girls, and I took this day as another opportunity to enjoy a lazy morning. My parents and the Kittlers had taken off much earlier to do some exploring. We agreed to meet at the beach.

In hindsight, if we wanted to end up all together, we should have started off that way. Apparently, none of us lives by the confines of practicality, so we went ahead with the "meet you there" plan and hoped for the best.

Any kind of separation for the kids was, of course, cause for alarm. Julia and Ally had no interest in being without their cousins at any time, much less at the beach, where frolicking in the sand and water was most enjoyable with kids their own age. But the adults of the group recognized that even the closest of kids need a break from each other every now and again.

"Do you want me to take your kids with us to the beach?" I asked Karla.

"I know that's what they'll want, but maybe we should divide and conquer for now. You know, so they'll better appreciate the afternoon and evening together."

Good thinking. The last thing I wanted was for the kids to tire of each other and look to the adults for entertainment.

Creating some breathing room between families every few days worked out very well. We got through the entire trip without any ornery bickering or hurt feelings. Family travelers will appreciate that a little alone time with your nuclear unit goes a long way in setting an affable tone when all the families converge.

Once settled at lovely Paradise Beach, we began to wonder if we had gotten our meeting location wrong. We walked the length of the beach several times to ensure that our party hadn't already arrived. There certainly was no chance we could miss our brood of Americans, so it was safe to say they were not there.

"Mom, what do you think is taking them so long?" Ally asked.

"I really don't know. They left the ship at least two hours before us. I fully expected them to be here when we arrived."

With no cell phones, we were at a loss.

What had happened to the rest of our family? Did they hop a shuttle gone rogue? We waited comfortably on the beach for at least an hour and a half. We grew increasingly concerned as the moments passed. The girls most especially, as they asked every fifteen minutes, "Where do you think they are?" "Do you think this is the right beach?" "How long are we going to stay if they don't show up?"

Oh God, I thought. *Please let them show up, PLEASE!*

Then, at long last, a silvery vision appeared in the distance, and I knew my Dad and his trademark head of white hair had arrived. I could spot him a mile away any day of the week.

Our excitement to see everyone was slightly offset by the arriving group's weary expressions and labored trek down the beach.

"Over here, over here!" Julia and Ally beckoned loudly while hands waved in the air. "Where have you been?"

The question loomed as we awaited the explanation.

"Give us a minute," Karla huffed. "It's been a long morning."

Once everyone had caught their breath and settled into a lounge chair, we learned that their commute to the beach had taken a wrong turn or two. Maybe even three. Early morning buses were few and far between at the hour the Kittlers and my parents left. Rather than go by way of a cab, Bob suggested they embark on an impromptu tour by foot.

His goal was to reach a more frequently traveled bus stop where they could jump on and ride to the beach, ultimately reducing their wait time. Much like the Pied Piper, Bob had his faithful followers eagerly in tow, as well as a few extra folks who thought Bob and the rest of the family were onto to something worthwhile. Soon, they all realized they were on a wild goose chase, trekking through a series of residential neighborhoods with no bus stops in sight. After far too long a morning stroll, they eventually found a bus, but were already tired before their day had even begun. When they made it to Paradise, they were drained and disgruntled.

Fortunately, Paradise is paradise. It didn't take long for the group to unwind and settle in to a lovely day at the beach. Greek beers found their way to the men, lapping ocean waves lured us in for several refreshing dips, and the prettiest straw umbrellas lined the shore to shade us from the sun.

The tropical look of these convenient sun savers added to the exotic and tranquil atmosphere. Food and drink were served right on the beach, and it was here that my father engaged in a lengthy conversation in Greek that went beyond the bargaining of the Athens Plaka. I suspect that the beautiful waitress had something to do with his crossover to the Greek side.

"Dad, I'm surprised you haven't been speaking Greek more," I said.

"It's been so long, Beth, I wasn't sure I could still carry on a conversation."

It was surprising to me that he felt that way after all the years he spoke Greek with my grandmother.

"Well, it was nice to hear you again," I said.

It was heartening to hear him go back and forth with the friendly waitress, and I could tell that he enjoyed it, too. I had no idea what they were talking about, which made me wish, more than ever, that I'd learned to speak the language when I was young. Learning to speak Greek was always on our radar, but the subject was never pushed. My father was the oldest and the only one of my grandmother's four sons who spoke Greek. He and my grandmother always had a special bond because of this. Realizing the exclusivity of this arrangement, I always wondered if Dad wanted Karla and me to understand Greek.

Even though I didn't understand my Dad and Yia Yia's conversations, I always knew when they were gossiping or talking directly about my sister or me. I now realize that my father and grandmother were quite cunning in their choice to slip into their language when it was convenient for them not to be understood. It was like a code language all their own, and it frustrates me to this day that I didn't try to crack it.

Conversely, if I ever really wanted to know what my father and grandmother were talking about, I could usually rely on my mother for a bit of intel. Even though she's Italian and doesn't speak either Italian or Greek, she had an uncanny way of knowing what my father was talking about, at least eighty percent of the time.

Back at Paradise Beach, our day turned out to be quite nice. We spent time in the water swimming, basking on rented floats, and soaking up the sun. We don't often go to the beach at home, so for us this was a treat.

"I have to say," Karla said, "despite the day's rocky start, I'm very glad we made it here. I don't remember enjoying a beach day like this since I was a teenager."

"I'll never forget you girls parking yourselves on the beach in Ogunquit right under the lifeguard chair, trying to get his attention," my dad said, repeating this story that I'd heard him tell so many times.

"Oh, please, let's not start down memory lane," I said. "I'm just glad the day ended better for all of you than it began."

I felt lucky to have avoided their morning struggle getting to the beach.

I soon realized, though, that luck is indeed a fickle mistress. Upon leaving the beach, we again decided to split up and go in different directions.

This time, Katherine joined Tony, Julia, Ally and me to explore more of Mykonos. We had a few hours to kill before we needed to be back at the ship and decided we would check out the downtown area. Katherine was the only one from the morning's aimless outing on foot who wasn't spent. Everyone else left the beach and headed directly back to the ship.

Much like all the little shops in Greece, those in Mykonos were adorable. We did begin seeing the same things repeatedly from one place to the next, but I enjoyed it nonetheless. The businesses, like the homes on our way to the beach, were all blue and white, small and intimate.

As time ticked by and we strolled about town, Tony alerted the rest of us that we best make our way to a stop where we could grab a shuttle service to the boat. Ah, those elusive shuttles. After ten-plus minutes of waiting around in a spot with no one else within eyeshot, I got impatient.

"Tony, we've got to be in the wrong place, there isn't a soul around us," I said.

"I don't know," he said. "I'm sure this is where I was told to go."

I don't often question Tony when it comes to directions because he usually knows exactly what he is doing, and I have the worst sense of direction. But something about this didn't seem right to me.

"We need to ask someone else," I pushed.

We found someone and were told, or so we thought, that we needed to walk about a mile to a transport station. The folks in Mykonos didn't speak strong English, as was the case in most of the other places we'd visited. The language barrier was suddenly a real problem. Where was my Greek-speaking dad when we needed him?

We decided to take the advice and walk to the "station." Our fingers were crossed that we'd not been led astray. We found it, but it looked abandoned, and we were told that the buses had stopped running ten minutes prior.

"Oh my God! You've got to be kidding me," I said out loud.

I tried to collect myself and remembered we could just find a taxi stand and hop a cab like we did earlier that morning. If we were lucky, Dimitri would reprise his role as driver.

Here's where lady luck let us down—big time. We walked another quarter mile to a taxi stand, where stood a line of about ten other misguided cruisers. These people were in the same time crunch, trying to make it back to the ship before it left port. Time was running out, and we were about a ten- or fifteen-minute drive away. At the infrequent rate cabs were coming, we would never make it back to the ship on time.

We were officially panicked.

"What are we going to do?" I said desperately to Tony.

"For the sake of the kids, we have to keep our cool," he whispered. "We'll figure this out."

He was outwardly optimistic, but I'm sure our dismayed expressions gave away our shared angst.

What in the world would happen if we missed the boat? I couldn't even fathom it.

"Let's go, ladies," Tony announced firmly. "We're going to have to walk."

"You can't be serious," I said, all composure lost. "It's too far."

"We have no other option. If we don't get moving *now*, we are going to be stranded here waiting for a cab to nowhere," Tony snapped.

The kids were bug-eyed and stood in stunned silence.

Poor Katherine.

As we began hoofing it, I could see the ship docked at port. The sight seemed promising, but it was still very far off for us to be able to get there in less than forty minutes. Would they hold the ship for us? We weren't alone, as others were walking, too, or should I say jogging, in the same direction. They were too far off to speak to, but before I could even contemplate catching up with anyone to commiserate, I realized that we were walking along a narrow, winding road, busy with cars. It felt like we were on a crash course for disaster.

We were on the left, the ocean side of the road. As cars moved speedily along to our right, I looked to the left only to see that the road on which we were running dropped off about one hundred feet, with no guardrail, right into the rocky ocean. As if worrying about making the ship weren't enough, now I was concerned about getting hit by a car or possibly slipping off the edge and plunging to my death. I focused on keeping the girls as safe as possible. If I screamed out, "Be careful!" one more time, I think someone would punch me.

"How did this happen?' I whined to Tony. "What made us think we could rely on a shuttle when we weren't even sure one existed?"

Tony was aggravated.

"Would you please stop talking and just keep walking?" he said.

About halfway to the ship, I seriously considered hitchhiking. And then, suddenly, a van drove by us, and someone glanced out and waved to Tony.

"Who the heck was that?" I said.

"I'm not sure," Tony said, looking longingly at the vehicle. I couldn't bother to wonder as we traversed this roadway to hell.

But then, like a rescue plane to a castaway, the van stopped ahead of us, and the driver began signaling us over to them. Next thing I knew, we'd hopped in, and in an instant our little nightmare was over. This was probably a horrible example to set for three young girls, but we were desperate.

"Jesus, Brian, you're the man!" Tony exclaimed when he entered the van. "You just saved us."

Brian? Who the hell is Brian?

"I didn't realize it was you until we passed you by," Brian said. "I knew you must need a ride because we've got about five minutes to board."

My heart was racing. It turned out Brian was a guy that Tony and Bob had been regularly gaming with at the ship's casino. Out of the goodness of his gambling heart, Brian told his driver to pick us up.

Karla and I had mocked Bob and Tony so many times, suggesting it was ridiculous that they felt the need to gamble every night as part of their vacation. We thought it was so frat-boyish and self-indulgent. Little did we know that their addictive behavior would be our saving grace.

Once back on the boat and reunited with the rest of our clan, we learned that the ship had alerted Karla and Bob of Katherine's absence. I was pleased to know that legitimate checks and balances were in place. According to Karla, Bob grabbed his and Katherine's passports and announced that if we weren't back in time he would take a passport in each hand and straddle the boat with one foot on the footbridge and one on land to strong-arm the ship from leaving. This sounded outrageous, and I'm certain it wouldn't have worked, but I loved his bravado and flair for the dramatic.

Histrionics aside, no one was really all that shaken up by our frantic arrival back on the ship. It was a "you had to be there" moment. If only they knew that we were walking inches away from the edge of a dangerous cliff with nothing but nothing to protect us. So much for a low-key day at the beach.

16. Damage Control

NO PLACE MORE THAN IN THE GREEK ISLANDS DID I wish for more time. Despite having experienced Mykonos in our own adventurous way, we weren't around long enough to get a feel for what it is best known for: its night life. Another time, perhaps—maybe without kids. For now, we were back on board our cruise ship, anticipating another full day at sea. Eleven days down, three to go.

"Where did the time go?" I said to Tony. "Do we really have only three days left?"

"Yup," Tony responded with a sigh. "I don't want to leave."

"Neither do I," I said, surprising myself.

I couldn't believe my ears. I always want to go home.

By now, we had already done and seen a lot. All told, we must have walked a marathon, and our brains were overflowing with newly acquired historical and cultural knowledge. Our bellies were just as full on foods so fabulous none of us could resist them. Little did we know that the best was yet to come.

Back on the ship, we'd taken advantage of almost all the amenities and features. But the one place I had avoided was the gym. I had come prepared for pretty much anything, including exercise, but I wasn't motivated. In fact, the thought of a workout had not even crossed my mind. Tony, on the other hand, took full advantage of the fitness center, which was well equipped and much larger than the dinky pool.

"You'd think they'd have given more square footage to the pool than the gym," I said to Tony.

"I totally disagree," said Tony. "I think the gym is more important than the pool."

Of course, he does—the quintessential contrarian.

"I don't know if the crowds of people crammed into the pools would agree, but okay."

When it comes to working out, Tony and I share the desire, but we have different mentalities with respect to approach. For as long as we've been together, we've both been into some fitness fad or another. Whether a spin class, step aerobics, or running miles to prepare for a triathlon, we've always stayed active and enjoyed it. We differ in that I don't want to exercise on vacation and Tony does. I also don't want to work out at crazy hours of the day.

"Hey, Beth, I'm going out for an early morning jog, you want to come?" Tony will ask at home.

"What time?"

"Five a.m."

"Are you serious? Definitely not."

Exercise on vacation is another exertion to which I am vehemently opposed.

Normally, I try to get in some kind of exercise about three or four times a week. But I find that as much as I want a break from the monotony of housecleaning, laundry, and cooking, I also like a break from exercise.

Tony is a bit more committed, and with his usually busy schedule at home, I suppose it's understandable. Although

I don't share Tony's laser focus when it comes to my fitness regime, I can respect that he'd want, or even enjoy, getting in some concentrated training without feeling rushed or having to squeeze it in at five in the morning or ten at night.

Our opposing views about working out fuel my top pet peeve when it comes to Tony's healthful devotion. It's not just that he's so dedicated to fitness that bugs me, but it's that he announces his plans to work out to anyone who'll listen.

"So, before the morning gets away from me, I'm going to head to the fitness center, okay?" he'll say.

"Okay, sounds good."

Twenty to thirty minutes later:

"I'm just going to fuel up and grab a bite to eat before I hit the gym."

"Yup, see you when you're done," I'll say, knowing full well it isn't over.

Thirty to forty minutes later:

"I'm so full from breakfast; I think I'm going to hold off on my work out until this afternoon."

"Just go already!"

I know that Tony's proclamations are a means of ensuring that he'll do what he says he's going to do. However, if I hear about his workout plans more than two times, I know he really doesn't want to do it. His procrastination is his subconscious secretly hoping that I'll suggest or even demand that he do something else so that he can blow off his workout without guilt.

Good God, I find it so annoying.

"If you're looking for me to put the kibosh on your work-out, you can forget it," I'll say. "Don't try to make me the bad guy—we both know you don't want to exercise, so just don't."

Don't get me wrong, I absolutely work out to stay fit. But more than any other reason, I exercise to clear my head and purge myself of the toxins, both physical and mental, that are polluting my body.

After eleven full days of pure excess, a feeling of toxicity overtook me on day twelve. I felt horrendous from gorging myself on way too many rich and wonderful foods. For God's sake, I thought I had gout! Not to mention the daily alcohol consumption to which I was entirely unaccustomed.

Walking, even the long distances we had, just wasn't enough to offset the debauchery. I was left with no other recourse than to get off my lounge chair and into the ship's fitness facility.

At this point I figured it would be good from a weight standpoint, but more importantly, it would boost my energy, which was in desperate need of a lift. I was so sluggish I honestly could have slept through the last three days of the trip.

My one set of workout clothes remained untouched at the bottom of my suitcase, along with my running sneakers. No one knew I had packed workout clothes. Tony may have mentioned to me several times that he was packing them, but I chose to keep mine to myself for fear of setting the expectation that I would use them.

The ship's gym was surprisingly busy. Apparently, more people were of Tony's mindset than I realized. The space was quite nice and had an air of luxury that I did not expect. The upscale setting made the idea of working out seem less of a chore and more of a treat. This was a nice change of pace, as opposed to my usual hole-in-the-wall kind of gym.

I discovered the Relaxation Room and the Persian Garden with steam, sauna, and mist and felt an excited, tingling sensation down my spine. It was so chichi and tempting in a high-maintenance, diva kind of way, and I found myself loving it. If ever I was to act and feel like a diva, vacation was the time.

I made my way over to the cardio section. To this day, and for as long as I have been going to gyms, I still find acquainting myself with new gym layouts and unfamiliar equipment intimidating. A fitness center staff member approached me.

"Can I assist you with any of the equipment?" he asked.

I thought about this for just a second. He was cute, and I could've easily said yes to delay my workout even longer. But as much as I despise the learning curve when trying out a new gym, I find working with a trainer even more annoying. I would much rather figure out what buttons to push on a machine by myself than have to stand awkwardly next to an instructor who's talking when I'm not listening.

"No thanks," I responded. "I'm good."

I knew from the moment I walked in that there was no better place for me than the treadmills. This was clear not because I desperately wanted to run, but because the treadmills were so nicely lined up against a wall of windows looking directly out to the tranquil blue water. I stepped onto my treadmill and couldn't help but pause to take it all in.

A fellow runner nearby took note.

"Pretty awesome, right?" she said.

"It really is," I answered. "I've done my fair share of running, but never like this."

"That glistening sea is the best motivation you could ask for," she said. "I would stay on this treadmill for days just to keep looking at this view."

Okay, she was clearly more excited to be here than I was, and I needed to get down to business.

"Yeah, I'll be lucky if I can push through thirty minutes."

In went my headphones, and go.

I began with a slow walk and gradually built up to a run. I thought ambitiously about sweating out all the bad while simultaneously drinking in the glorious view that flowed past. There was almost something spiritual about it.

With my music blasting, all else was tuned out, and suddenly I felt completely alone. I couldn't see the people behind me and those alongside me had disappeared from view. I was in the zone, and I couldn't have enjoyed it more.

Periodically I would get a dizzy feeling. I'd give my head a shake and look down only to find myself nearly off the treadmill.

"Be careful," said my running neighbor. "I've seen people run themselves right off these things."

"Right, thanks," I said, really wishing she'd stop talking to me.

It didn't occur to me that I needed to be paying closer attention to what I was doing. With each step I took, there was a millisecond when I'd be airborne, meanwhile the boat continued to move under me. As a result, my body position on the treadmill would shift ever so slightly. It was a weird sensation, and being conscious of it made the run even better.

About twenty minutes in, the novelty of this new running experience wore off, and I realized how very far I'd let myself go on this trip. I was feeling every appetizer, heavy entrée, and dessert I'd eaten. It was as if every one of them were in a pack on my back.

For the most part, I pay attention to eating right, but like so many women, I'm never satisfied. There is never a time when I don't wish I was five pounds lighter. But those five, sometimes six, sometimes seven pounds are impossible to lose no matter how hard I try. That number had to be up to at least ten pounds by now.

It is beyond frustrating that nothing, no new workout or diet, seems to propel my body into any kind of change. My challenge to any fitness and nutrition professional out there is to figure out a way to help me with the impossible task of losing those stubborn pounds and inches that have haunted me ever since having children. I'm convinced it can't be done.

I doubt that this one run undid much of my physical damage; however, my mental state was so greatly improved that I nearly broke my conviction not to brag about my exercise accomplishments. I felt so energized and purged that I was compelled to preach the values of a good workout to all who would listen. I opted not to go that route, but when I was asked what I thought of the gym, I did say, "I wish I'd gone sooner."

17. Naples

"THIS IS IT," TONY LAMENTED, "OUR LAST DAY."

"How is that possible?" I asked. "I feel like we just got here. I honestly don't want it to end."

I'd fallen into such a groove that the thought of returning to life as usual was depressing. I was so distanced from the responsibilities of home that any lingering worries about things left undone or issues unaddressed were completely forgotten. It was hard to believe I was the same person who'd been panicked over so much time away from home. What was I thinking? I was so immersed in this experience that I wasn't even concerned about the flight home. I was happy, really happy to be doing what we were doing.

My most highly anticipated sight in this port was Pompeii. Despite having viewed so many ruins already, I was particularly interested in the story of Pompeii. As a child, I recall having seen images of men, women, children, and animals who had been frozen in time beneath the encapsulating ash. The preservation of these bodies, so clearly captured in motion and distress, was shocking. The idea that the unforgiving gasses and debris from Mount Vesuvius spewed out so quickly and furiously that these poor souls had no chance of escape was unsettling to me as a child. I looked forward to walking through the site to help me better understand how those chilling events unfolded in AD 79.

It seems that whenever I really want to do something, we inevitably get sidetracked, and my wish list is the one tossed out the window. In this case, I couldn't blame any one person; it was out of our control, due to traffic. In one day, we had four major stops to make, and something had to give. Unfortunately, it was Pompeii. I treated the disappointment as another good reason to return someday.

Our day turned out to be so fulfilling that I couldn't complain. I was happy enough to see the ominous Mount Vesuvius from a relatively short distance. Its dark, towering presence, in the middle of such a highly populated area, was powerful on its own.

"I'm bummed that we aren't going to make it to Pompeii, but at least we got to see Vesuvius," I said to Karla.

"Vesuvius?" Karla balked with total authority. "That's not Vesuvius."

"What are you talking about?" I responded quizzically, confused. "It's not?"

I questioned myself because Karla was so secure in her response.

"Am I losing my mind?" I said to her. "I know that's Vesuvius."

"No, it isn't! Oh wait, you're right," she said, just as confidently and unapologetically as she had in the first place. "That is Vesuvius."

"Oh my God, who does that?"

I liked my sister's total confidence in what she was saying. Even when she's one hundred percent wrong, she believes and speaks as though she's one hundred percent right. There is something appealing about that kind of unabashed conviction. One of my uncles used to say about my Yia Yia, "Ma may not always be right . . . but she's never wrong." Karla is just like my grandmother.

Vesuvius and Pompeii aside, Naples, Sorrento, and the Amalfi Coast fit perfectly into our agenda, and each location made our final day a perfect case of ending on a high note.

Domenico

Our adventure in southern Italy was almost as much about our guide as it was about the places we visited. Domenico was a tour guide extraordinaire who added tremendously to our final impressions of the Mediterranean.

An attractive Italian man in his thirties, Domenico was not exceptionally tall, but he held himself with an air of confidence. His dark complexion, styled black hair, pristine wardrobe, bright smile, and gentle eyes made him easy to look at.

He was beautiful on the inside as well. During the first fifteen minutes we spent with him, we learned that his charm and charisma couldn't be rivaled.

"I love this guy," I whispered to Karla. "He's sweet and hilarious at the same time."

"He certainly is a character," she replied.

While we spent more time than we'd have liked in our tour vehicle getting from one destination to the next, we could not have asked for better entertainment along the way. Domenico was informative, funny, and the epitome of a poised, passionate, and brutally honest Italian man.

Our Naples outing began with a ride to the quaint seaside town of Sorrento. The ride itself was the opening act that led up to the main attraction.

Our group of ten split into two vans. Karla and I didn't realize at the time that our decision to hop into Domenico's van was ideal in every way. The four kids joined us, and while that may have seemed like the short end of the stick, it was nice that Karla and I were the only adults on which Domenico would focus his energy. Essentially, we had him all to ourselves, which would be an unforgettable bonus.

No offense to the men in my family, but had they been there, they'd have undoubtedly monopolized the conversation. We wouldn't have had the pleasure of the unfiltered, unedited Domenico that we were lucky to experience.

Alex had the good fortune of sitting up front with Domenico as we rode to our various stopping points for the day. This spot gave Alex not only a bird's eye view but also a targeted delivery of the many life lessons that Domenico decided to share. While Karla and I admired the gorgeous scenery of lemon trees and sunflower fields outside of the moving van's windows, Alex was schooled on what it meant to be a real man—Domenico-style.

Most memorable was Domenico's advice to Alex on how best to approach life. For an impressionable fifteen-year-old boy, the timing of such a conversation couldn't have been better. Charmingly, Domenico referred to Alex as Alessandro, not for any other reason than because he wanted to.

"Alessandro," Domenico began emphatically. "Lesson number one—listen to what I tell you. Don't worry about tomorrow. Tomorrow doesn't exist, there is only today. It's the Italian way."

This was the first of at least a dozen Domenico lessons we all had the pleasure of hearing.

This was a direct response to Alex questioning his mother regarding when his next meal would be and where he would get it.

I nearly melted as I realized how very true Domenico's statement was, whether about food or life's more pressing issues. We so often let the precious present slip by as we lament our past or fear our future.

Domenico's words of wisdom did not end there. He went on to quiz Alex about his dating status, which completely horrified my typically teen nephew. Poor Alex was completely disinterested in having any kind of conversation about girls in front of his aunt and mother, but boy, was it funny to watch.

Domenico also shared how he came to be such a masterful tour guide. It didn't come easily, he told us, but as with most success stories, perseverance and strength helped him through tough times. He shared that a business partner had once cheated him and left him with nothing.

"I was broken," Domenico said. "Broken on the floor."

To hear him share this struggle was a bit heart-wrenching, even for someone I barely knew. But that was what was appealing about him. He put himself totally out there. He was an open book with what seemed like an infinite amount of knowledge and wisdom to share. We were like sponges, just soaking it all in.

In direct contrast to Domenico's sad story about falling on hard times, he quickly turned the conversation to the excitement and joy he experienced when he came through this difficult period and found himself happier than he'd ever been. It was like being on an emotional roller-coaster, and I loved the thrill.

On his upswing, we learned that Domenico had founded the touring company in which we were so pleasurably partaking, simply named "Private Tour in Italy." He proudly showed us various business card prototypes to get our opinion. His enthusiasm was contagious and adorable. We even caught the three girls giggling coyly a few times at the engaging chatter.

This may have been their reaction when Domenico went on to tell us that with his financial windfall from the success of the touring company, he would like to do two things. First, he planned to launch a chocolate business, and second, he would like to invest in a tan and brown motorcycle. Domenico further explained that he loved motorcycles and his favorite colors were tan and brown.

"Tan and brown?" I said out loud. "How can those be your favorite colors?"

How could someone with such a colorful personality love tan and brown? I thought.

"These are the colors of the earth and men," Domenico said. "They are manly."

I wasn't about to question his manliness, so I took him at his word.

This vivacious Italian man with so many charismatic layers and a passion for life was a true personality. I loved everything about him but recognized that his fervor was most likely a good thing and a bad thing all at once. My own Mediterranean mix leaves me with a temperament that is, at times, volatile. I have learned to temper my hotheaded outbursts over the years, but if pushed, I can erupt much like Mount Vesuvius did nearly two thousand years ago. The flip side of explosive personalities is that the fun side can be so much fun and so very engaging, like Domenico, but the dark side can surface in an instant.

I caught a glimmer of this with Domenico on two occasions. The first occurred when were stuck in traffic. Out of nowhere Domenico decided to flag down a random motorcyclist going in the opposite direction to determine the cause of the holdup. Once he got his information he let out his frustration by yelling in Italian to anyone who would listen, all the while flailing his arm out the window in a stereotypical, Italian-talking-with-their-hands kind of way.

"I obviously don't know what he's saying," Karla whispered with raised eyebrows. "But if I were to guess it involves an 'F' and a 'you' in various iterations."

"He's feisty," I said with a devilish smirk.

In another unexpected turn that demonstrated the fury that lies within, there was a moment when we'd stopped to take a scenic photo and Domenico realized he had dirt on the bottom of his tan pants.

"Oh my God," he shouted, "look at my pants, they are filthy. How did this happen? What is on my pants?" All the while he furiously brushed at the stain with the hope that it would disappear.

I couldn't help but laugh and make eyes with my sister since, number one, I couldn't even see the dirt and two, his reaction seemed a little excessive.

"Domenico, your pants look fine. Really, it's not even noticeable," I offered, hoping to make him feel better.

"No, no!" he said. "I can't be out like this. Excuse me a minute."

I didn't know where he was off to, but when he returned, he was wearing new pants. I couldn't stop smiling. Something about it was utterly ridiculous.

Domenico had resolved his pants problem by changing into a clean pair he kept in the trunk of the car for such emergencies. At least he was well prepared to meet his funnily fastidious standards.

Before reaching our first destination for the day, Domenico decided to give us a coffee break at a friend's convenience store. At this point, we were no longer caravanning with the other car transporting Tony, Bob, and my parents. I'm not sure what they were doing when Domenico decided it was time for a caffeine fix, but those of us on Team Domenico were perfectly comfortable with being derailed.

It was an ordinary looking convenience store that sold coffee and other provisions. Shelves were stocked with typical sundries and snacks, and the register counter looked just as you might expect. We were inside for only a moment before Domenico instructed us to take a seat across the street.

"Go, sit there, relax," he said while pointing somewhere out the door. "I'll bring you something nice."

I hadn't even noticed that a place across the street existed, but indeed it did, and we made our way over to a lovely outdoor table situated on a small grass common area. We overlooked the crisp blue ocean, boats in motion leaving frothy wakes and picturesque rocky cliffs that seemed to encase everything in their shadow. Suddenly, our pit stop was a divine detour. Had we driven by, I never would have noticed it.

In a matter of moments, we were sipping delicious cappuccinos with decorative latte art. Domenico also hand delivered the yummiest little almond candies and sweet cakes. He was a man in charge, and he aimed to please.

Caffeine and sweets are never a bad way to start when it comes to making a woman happy. All that was missing was a bouquet of flowers. Karla doesn't even drink coffee, yet this was a treat she couldn't pass up. We sat contentedly while looking out at the boats and enjoying our beverages and confections.

"Where did Domenico go?" Karla asked.

"Good question—maybe he needed some time to collect himself after the pants incident."

Sorrento

In due time, both vans reconvened in the upscale town of Sorrento. We met up and wasted no time walking, shopping, and letting the beauty of the town sink in before we ventured off for a lunch that would leave an indelible mark on our memories.

Sorrento was a delightful little coastal town. It was not crowded, and every lemon and orange tree we passed was like seeing the Eiffel Tower for the first time. There was something so simple and lovely about these fruit trees growing every which way we turned. They certainly reminded me that we were not in New England anymore. Sidewalk fruits stands, buildings painted in lemon yellow, and outdoor cafés were all part of this perfect cliffside setting.

As we poked around shops featuring artwork, jewelry, and trinkets, I couldn't get my mind off my Mediterranean mission, which was to return home with a fabulous pair of

European shoes.

It was now or never. So, in Sorrento, I truly channeled my inner Carrie Bradshaw. I stumbled upon a few shoe shops that had nice options, but it wasn't until I walked into a tiny little shoetique called Balducci's that I knew I'd found the right place.

The smell of wood and leather hung in the air as my eyes fell upon the prettiest footwear I'd seen so far on the trip. Those that caught my eye were elegantly glitzy and colorful. All were well-made and crafted with obvious care. I had no doubt that I would find a pair of authentic Italian heels here. The problem came when trying to figure out which ones to choose. Thankfully, I had a glam squad in tow.

"Girls, which ones do you like?" I said to Julia, Ally, and Katherine.

A loaded question to a group of teen and preteen girls—I should've known they wouldn't agree.

"The blue ones," said Julia.

"No, those are boring. Get the red ones," said Ally

"How about these?" Katherine suggested while holding a pretty yellow pair up for view.

"This is going to be harder than I thought," I said.

"Come on, Mom," said Julia. "Just get the ones I like. I'll be first in line to wear them anyway."

That's my girl.

Eventually, I made a choice. They are delicate, pink, and oh-so-fun. It was an indulgence that was well worth the wait and money. Sometimes being frivolous pays off in pure joy and satisfaction, and I love having a memento from this quaint town. God, I love shoes!

If we weren't about to travel up a mountainside to land at our lunch spot, I may very well have put the shoes right on my feet. But to be safe, I kept them in the box for a more suitable occasion. Every time I wear my Balducci's, I smile with nostalgia for this special town with great shoes, great views, and great memories.

Amalfi Coast/Positano

LUNCH IS A MEAL THAT SEEMS MORE A NECESSITY than a luxury. I am by no means the kind of lady who lunches back home. While I envy those who regularly gather for long midday meals comprised of some lunch, but mostly wine, that's just not me. I typically rush through lunch while standing over my sink, just to fuel up and get ready for the next thing on my to-do list. But when you are traveling the Amalfi Coast with Domenico, there is no better time to indulge.

"I'm going to take you some place special for lunch," Domenico told us.

Okay, sounds good, I thought.

I expected nice, but not in my wildest imagination did I envision what we got. Domenico and his counterpart, Rafael, chauffeured us to an eatery that we never could've found on our own. On our way there, we all made a quick stop for a stunning photo op with the Amalfi Coast as our backdrop.

Dramatic rocky cliffs, whitecapped waters, distant rooftops, and colorful pink flowers framed the family photo that would set the stage for what was to come. It felt like we'd driven for miles upward when we finally arrived at a one-of-a-kind dining spot nestled atop the small mountain.

Located in the town of Positano, the unassuming little restaurant was named Fattoria la Tagliata, and the moment we arrived, every one of my senses went into overdrive.

I was immediately enamored with the beautiful red flowers that lined the front of the restaurant. They were dense and rich in color with a pleasant, subtle aroma. Before we even reached the entrance, my senses of sight and smell were delightfully engaged.

The restaurant itself had a natural, rustic appeal. Wooden timbers that appeared to have been chopped and used in their raw form reinforced the structure, while stone walking paths, secured with an attractive combination of moss and cement, led the way to the most unexpected dining room. We were visually charmed by the decorative tiles embedded in the exterior walls. I ran my hand across their smooth surface while feeling the uneven stones underfoot. A peek into the tiny bathroom revealed equal care and craftsmanship. The blue and yellow tiles popped in a way that made even the powder room look special.

We entered the dining room with Domenico leading the way. He took the opportunity to enter first, letting his "people" know that we'd arrived. We got situated at our table and hoped that Domenico and Rafael would sit with us.

"Please join us," Bob and Tony beckoned. "We insist."

But like every other gracious guide before them, they politely declined.

"No, no," said Domenico. "We don't eat, we wait for you. Be with your family and enjoy!"

Although they didn't accept our invitation, Domenico and Rafael hung close by without ever taking a seat. They maintained a short distance for the entire two hours we were there and managed to be part of our conversation nearly the entire time. The pleasure was all ours.

Our table might as well have been outdoors. We were seated on a covered deck with nothing but sheer curtains and log supports between us and the steep drop down the mountainside. The room was full of other patrons. Those afraid of heights might not have had the stomach to take in the spectacular ocean view, but it took our breath away.

The only remaining senses to be tantalized were taste and hearing, and we didn't have to wait long for the full sensory experience. The moment we were all comfortably seated, we were inundated with food, in the best way possible. We didn't order one thing; it was all brought to us. Whatever the chef was cooking was what was served, and we thoroughly enjoyed it.

Every plate was also a work of art: each was hand-painted, colorful, and artistic. And before we knew it, music filled the air when the owner's niece took a microphone and asked all the patrons to join in on a sing-along.

"Oh fun! Come on, everybody grab an instrument," Karla shouted enthusiastically.

"What's going on?" my dad said, confused at the sudden hoopla.

Not everyone was as excited about the impromptu jam session as was my sister.

All the kids were handed musical instruments and asked to join the singer. There were several reluctant expressions, but in YOLO (You Only Live Once) spirit, we all went along with it.

The kids hopped up, some hesitantly, while everyone else in the restaurant rose to clap and groove to the music. The Italian blond beauty entertained us with her soothing voice, ethnic songs, and gregarious hospitality. I suspect Domenico and Rafael also appreciated the show, as they didn't take their eyes off the singer for a minute. I don't think I saw Domenico smile quite as widely as he did while watching her. The entire scene was electric.

Her rousing renditions of both familiar and unfamiliar songs left us ready to sit back and enjoy the end of our memorable meal. Served family style, it was a meal that included five appetizers, five entrees, homemade wine, pear grappa, and five desserts. It was extravagant, yet unpretentious.

As desserts and limoncello came to the table, so did the owner–chef. She was an older Italian woman wearing a kerchief to cover her head and a dish towel slung over her shoulder. Domenico lovingly suggested that we refer to her as "Mama." She and her husband explained how this family-run restaurant came to be and how everyone from the singer to the waiter was a member of their family. Everything about this place was full of love. Every bite that was served was natural and simply prepared, yet it was the most delicious food I'd ever eaten.

As we left, full of food and drink, we walked out a different way than we came in. Our exit out the back door led us to the family's garden where the fresh herbs that so deliciously flavored our meal were grown. I admired the uniformity of the thriving plantings and the vibrancy of the foliage. It made me envy the Italian climate.

The chirp of a little pet bird, caged on the side of the garden, was a nice distraction for the kids. There were new things to see with every step we took, but our moment in time at this special place had come to an end. Domenico and Rafael rallied the troops to load back up into the vehicles.

"Don't forget these," Domenico said while handing two wine bottles to Bob and Tony.

Several bottles of house wine had been served as part of the dining experience, but we'd reached our tipping point and just couldn't finish.

"We can take them with us?" Bob asked.

"Yes, of course," said Domenico. "Take it. You drink later."

You've got to love Italy. Domenico certainly didn't have to say that twice. Bob and Tony took off with the remaining bottles, which I suspected they would demolish on the way to our next destination. Shockingly, they ended up saving the wine to enjoy at another time.

At this point our expectation was that we would move on to see Pompeii, but here we learned time and traffic would not allow it. Never one to disappoint, Domenico devised an alternate plan. What would a good tour guide be without a few surprises up his sleeve?

He took a detour to a "locals only" beach with the intention of giving us some relief from the heat and traffic. In no time, we found ourselves with sand beneath our toes in a small but busy alcove full of beach-goers tucked away behind tall rocky cliffs. It was jam-packed with young Italians swimming and playing beach games. We probably looked completely out of place, but with Domenico by our side, I felt comfortable and confident that we'd be accepted. It seemed that no matter where we were, Domenico had a pal who would pave the way for us to partake in true Italian culture.

We had come prepared with bathing suits and gladly took advantage of the refreshing break. Domenico remained on the sideline with his long pants, dress shirt, and fancy watch. It had to be one hundred degrees, yet our cool tour guide remained just that, cool and debonair.

A quick stop at the snack bar and we thought we'd be good to go. As we gathered amid the crowd for gelato and a cool beer for Bob and Tony, we waited patiently and comfortably for Domenico's word that it was time to go. Following a brief bathroom break, Ally arrived in tears.

"Mom!" she wailed. "I was locked in the bathroom for like ten minutes. I couldn't get out and I was screaming, and no one could hear me."

I knew that she'd been in the ladies room for less than five minutes, but I indulged her mild hysteria nonetheless.

"My poor baby!" I said. "What happened, how did you get out?"

"Papou finally heard me and opened the door," she said.

"Oh, thank goodness. Where's Papou now?"

"I don't know," Ally said in her often used yet rarely needed exasperated voice.

The good news was that Dad hadn't gone missing since Athens. The bad news was that by this time we realized he'd already been gone for about ten minutes and we were ready to leave. We began thinking about drawing straws to choose which family member would go find him. We wisely gave it just a couple more minutes, and in good-old-Dad fashion, he arrived, as we all knew he eventually would. This time he looked annoyed.

Ally ran up to him and demanded, "Papou, where did you go?"

"After I got you out of the bathroom, I went in and got locked in, too," he said with a look and tone of total frustration.

On that note, we left.

18. Reflection

OUR TIME IN NAPLES CAME TO A BITTERSWEET END
with hugs and cheers for Domenico and his cohort, Rafael.

"Talk about saving the best for last," I said. "I cannot think
of a better way to have spent our last day. Domenico, you
were the best!"

"It's all of you who made it special," he said. "Because you
wanted it to be."

I just loved him. He was so cute.

I thought about what he said and appreciated the mes-
sage. I don't think there has ever been a time when I've
been so open to the good things around me. Everyone in
my family, kids included, were equally receptive. I hoped
that we would not leave this energy behind. It felt good to
be excited and engaged in everything we were doing, seeing,
and experiencing.

While our spiritual energy was at an all-time high, our
physical energy was low. We were all exhausted by the end of
this extraordinary, fun-filled day. As we wearily made our way
back on the ship and to our cabins, there was a mood of quiet
contentment. Our last day of touring was done. I hoped we
would not experience a letdown of having nothing more to
look forward to.

"Can you believe we all got up to sing with that lady at the restaurant?" Alex remarked.

"Oh my God, I know," said Julia. "At first, I was so embarrassed, but then I was like, who cares? I'm never going to see any of these people again, and they were way more into it than we were, anyway."

"I think this was my favorite day," Ally added. "Because everyone was really nice, and Domenico was funny."

"Me too," said Katherine. "Every day I've thought that was the best day and then the next day happens and it's even better."

Were my ears deceiving me, or could these children be getting it . . . understanding that you should embrace life, make the most of whatever you're doing and appreciate it?

I realized we had so many "trip moments" to rehash, relive, and remember that it might be months or years before any feelings of letdown would set in. By that time, I was sure something else new and exciting would fill the void.

We had one night left to savor the happenings of the last two weeks. Despite feeling drained, we knew we could not miss this last chance to cruise the Mediterranean in style.

I readied myself for one more meal out and about on the Celebrity Equinox. After a quick glance at my tired face in the mirror, I vowed to return home to a week's worth of cereal for dinner without makeup, in my jammies, on my couch. I thought this would be an acceptable recovery from this lavish lifestyle I'd so enjoyed.

At seven p.m. on the nose, we heard a rap at our door and welcomed my sister, Bob, and the kids into our suite as we put the final touches on our evening outfits. Tony donned a blue and white Greek-style tunic he'd purchased in the Plaka in Athens. He wore it proudly, if not a bit smugly, and we all gave a giggle at his ongoing zeal for embracing the culture, no matter where we were.

My parents heard the hullabaloo and joined us.

"Hey, Tony," said Dad. "How about some Ouzo to go along with your shirt?"

Tony's eyes lit up.

"Absolutely, Dad. But before that, let's have a toast here in the room."

Out came one of the leftover bottles of wine from lunch in Positano. I knew they wouldn't go to waste.

We gathered all the glasses we could find and emptied the bottle so that everyone would have at least a sip, even the kids. What the heck? We were in European waters.

With glasses raised, we collectively clinked and cheered.

"To an amazing trip," we said to one another.

"*Opa!*" Tony inserted. Of course, he did—at least he didn't say *grazie* or *prego*.

"A trip of a lifetime!" my mom ended.

We emptied our glasses and prepared for one last walk to the dining room.

Assembled at our usual table in the formal dining room, we were warmly greeted by our regular waitress.

"Angel," Bob called. "This is our final meal together. We'll miss you."

"Yes, Bob, I'll miss you too and your lovely family," she said. "You were my favorite table by far."

"Oh, come on, I'm sure you say that to all of your guests," said Bob coyly.

If Angel's mission was to make every table she served feel like they were her one and only, she certainly accomplished that with us. It helped that Bob chatted her up like she was a celebrity on *Inside the Actors Studio* and he was the host, James Lipton.

To our credit, particularly Bob's, we all took time to engage the ship's crew in conversation. It was interesting to learn where they were from and what it was like for them to live on a cruise ship. We not only got a peek into the worlds of these multicultural young people, but the connections enriched our travel experience on a deeper, more personal level. It's amazing how well you can get to know people in two short weeks if you make the effort.

We were lucky to have had so many great servers and stewards who humored us and took our attention away from one another every now and again. Maybe it wasn't luck so much as good karma. I suspect we received the good treatment we did because we valued and respected the quality service we were offered. If I've learned nothing else in my limited travels, it's that being a gracious guest and treating those who are assisting you with kindness and respect is paramount to a positive travel experience. Leave any negativity at home. It's not welcome on vacation.

I'm eternally grateful to have made this trip with my family who share in my appreciation and admiration for those who assisted us along the way.

At the table, there was an air of total fulfillment as we all nibbled on our last meal. Although still full from our extravagant lunch, I didn't want to miss my last chance to indulge, so I ordered an elegant surf and turf plate that satisfied my every taste bud. Good God, I'm a glutton.

"I can't believe you're ordering something so rich after today's lunch," Mom said.

"I know, but I want to close out this vacation with a bang. Stay tuned, because I'm ordering dessert, too."

"Yes!" said Ally. That child has never turned down a chance at dessert.

I took my time and savored every bite. Not just because I wanted to remember the fabulous tastes, but because I was still so full I could barely get the food down.

I enjoyed it nonetheless, and we took the extra time to debate whether we were happy or sad to be heading home in the morning.

"One of the things that I'll miss the most is having someone cook for me every single day," said Karla. "This was pure heaven; it makes me want a personal chef."

I knew exactly what she was talking about. As the one who does all the cooking in my family but is by no means a passionate cook, this culinary escape was over-the-top fabulous for me, too.

"I'm just happy I got to see so many incredible places and countries," said Tony. "This makes me want to travel even more."

Uh-oh. I hoped I would come away with a new affinity for travel, because something told me that this trip had started an obsession. I could tell Tony was on a travel high, and it wouldn't be easy to bring him down.

"I'll miss spending so much wonderful time with my family," said my mom. "As marvelous as the places were that we visited, nothing compares to seeing my precious grandchildren and beautiful family every day."

"Awww—so sweet, Mom."

We raised our glasses in a farewell toast that seemed to perfectly wrap up our trip.

Even though I was lamenting leaving, I couldn't deny that the comforts of home were calling my name. I was just about ready. My bags were packed, and I found my mind periodically wandering to the juicy gossip I was sure to come home to. I might even admit to a twinge of anxious excitement.

Two of my favorite things following a trip are unpacking and reorganizing my routine life. As boring as it may sometimes feel, I love getting my normal life back into order and getting caught up on what I've missed. I enjoy returning to the trivial chitter-chatter that I was so anxious to leave behind in the first place. Escaping the day-to-day drivel for two weeks is just enough time to make coming back to it tolerable.

We went to bed that night knowing we'd sleep soundly. Our bodies were tired and there were no new adventures to look forward to. I was even too tired to worry about the plane ride.

We awoke one last time to the sound of the ship being secured to the dock. This time, we did not fall back to sleep. Tony and I lay in bed, eyes open, waiting.

"I thought you'd be jumping for joy to be going home, but you're not," he said.

"I'm sad to say goodbye," I said. "This trip far exceeded my expectations."

If only I could take the wonderful tour guides and other esteemed folks who we were so lucky to encounter back home with me. So much of the trip was defined by these wonderful people, and more specifically, the European way of life they embodied. It was the perceived European lifestyle that I was caught up in. The relaxed pace and unaffected mentality of the European people was enviable, and so drastically different from our norm. If I could take home only one souvenir, it would be this.

I recognize that this "lifestyle" I was stalking was merely a surface-level peek at a charmed reality. I'm sure the beautiful people of Italy, Greece, and Turkey are in many ways just like us in America. They wish for things they don't have while we admire what they do have. I suppose nothing is ever perfect, but enjoying a different way of life was certainly eye-opening and in many ways life-changing.

"What was your biggest takeaway from this trip?" Tony asked me.

"There are two things, actually," I said. "First is that we eat like crap at home. The food here was so phenomenal—fresh and unprocessed. I know that has to be a better way to eat and live, and I want to do more of that."

"I completely agree," Tony said. "This was the best food I've eaten in my life."

Coming from him, that was a big statement.

"Right, which leads me to my second point," I said. "We are way too caught up in 'busier is better.' I can't stand it—we are always rushing around like chickens with our heads cut off. We need to slow down."

This trip changed me in many ways. Most significant was my renewed appreciation of the pleasures and benefits of travel. I was now more willing to say yes to Tony's travel whims. If this trip was any indicator, I knew I would gain so much pleasure and personal growth by reintroducing travel to my life. To travel with my children was a gift that even I couldn't shy away from.

Following our trip to the Mediterranean, Tony and I decided to sell our Lake Winnipesaukee vacation home of fifteen years with the express purpose of traveling more.

"Why did you sell that place?" friends asked. "It was such a nice getaway."

"It was time," I said. "We need the flexibility to do other things."

There were periodic moments of seller's remorse, and we worried we'd miss it. Not until I reached out to Julia and Ally's summer camp counselor, Sue, did I know we'd made the right choice.

"Sue," I said, "I am sorry to say that the girls will not be returning to camp this year. We have decided to sell our lake house in favor of traveling to more distant places."

"That is bad but good news!" Sue answered. "I'm sad that the girls won't be around anymore, but I have to agree that traveling is the best thing to do. I learned more traveling than I ever did in all of my years at school."

Now when Tony or the girls suggest a new place to visit, I listen instead of running from the conversation.

Today, our travel sights are set on Portugal, Spain, Paris, a Viking River Cruise, and most definitely a return to Italy. I'm fortunate and thankful to have the opportunity to explore the world and to have children and family who are willing and able to share the experience with me.

My fear of flying is not gone, but if this trip taught me nothing else, it's that the beauty of the places I might visit is far more powerful than my fear of getting there.

Not long after we got home, Tony approached me excitedly. "You will not believe the trip Sam just told me about. I'm looking into it right now."

Dammit, Sam!

I admit my heart skipped a little before I caught myself. I certainly didn't rush into a response with a resounding yes, but this time, I took a deep breath and didn't say no.

Acknowledgements

MY DEEPEST GRATITUDE GOES OUT TO MY FAMILY and friends. Your support and encouragement has meant the world to me. Thank you Emilie-Noelle Provost for being my first editor and more so writing coach. Lisa Bernard, I have valued your feedback and kind words greatly—proofreading on the lanai never sounded so good. Ken Bonin, your artistic talent knows no bounds, thank you for making this cover so special and equal appreciation to Steve Pennimpede for bringing the art to life in color. Emily O'Brien (photographer) and Lysa Pelletier-Gibbs (stylist) you are my sisters in creativity. I never imagined taking a headshot could be such fun. Thank you to my E. L. Marker editor, Tamara Heiner, it was a pleasure working with you and thank you WiDo Publishing and E. L. Marker for making this little book of mine a reality.

About the Author

BETH DAIGLE IS A LIFELONG NEW ENGLANDER residing north of Boston with her husband and daughters. Prior to settling into her role as a writer, Beth was a marketing professional whose favorite part of the job was writing. As a freelancer, Beth has enjoyed contributing to numerous lifestyle and home publications, yet she yearned for something more than a magazine article. Then along came *Musing Mediterranean*. Beth quickly became immersed in chronicling this travel event and articulating her perceptions of the places she visited, the people she met, the foods she enjoyed and the crazy moments she encountered. The idea that someone who may never travel to Greece, Italy or Turkey could appreciate this experience through Beth's eyes became a driving force behind the story. Revealing her struggle with travel anxiety helped Beth move forward and embrace, once again, how very wonderful it is to travel the world.

"The world is a book, and those who do not travel read only one page." St. Augustine.

Beth is a creative soul who finds joy in art, home design, gardening, reading, writing, a good laugh and an even better television show.

Website:	BethDaigle.com
Blog:	3OlivesandaTwist.com
Instagram:	3olivesandatwist
Facebook:	@3olivesandatwist
Twitter:	@3olivesnatwist